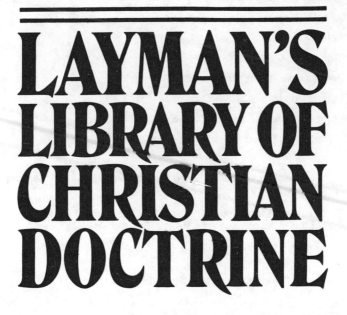

LAYMAN'S LIBRARY OF CHRISTIAN DOCTRINE

The Nature of God

FISHER HUMPHREYS

BROADMAN PRESS
Nashville, Tennessee

4216-34

ISBN: 0-8054-1634-X

Dewey Decimal Classification: 231

Subject Heading: GOD

Library of Congress Catalog Card Number: 84-20037

Printed in the United States of America

Unless otherwise indicated, Scripture quotations are from the King James Version of the Bible.

Scripture quotations marked (RSV) are from the Revised Standard Version of the Bible, copyrighted 1946, 1952, © 1971, 1973.

Library of Congress Cataloging in Publication Data

Humphreys, Fisher.
  The nature of God.

  (Layman's library of Christian doctrine ; v. 4)
  Includes index.
  1. God.   2. Trinity.   3. Theology, Doctrinal—
Popular works.   4. Baptists—Doctrines.   I. Title.
II. Series.
BT102.H85   1985   231   84-20037
ISBN 0-8054-1634-X

Foreword

The *Layman's Library of Christian Doctrine* in sixteen volumes covers the major doctrines of the Christian faith.

To meet the needs of the lay reader, the *Library* is written in a popular style. Headings are used in each volume to help the reader understand which part of the doctrine is being dealt with. Technical terms, if necessary to the discussion, will be clearly defined.

The need for this series is evident. Christians need to have a theology of their own, not one handed to them by someone else. The *Library* is written to help readers evaluate and form their own beliefs based on the Bible and on clear and persuasive statements of historic Christian positions. The aim of the series is to help laymen hammer out their own personal theology.

The books range in size from 140 pages to 168 pages. Each volume deals with a major part of Christian doctrine. Although some overlap is unavoidable, each volume will stand on its own. A set of the sixteen-volume series will give a person a complete look at the major doctrines of the Christian church.

Each volume is personalized by its author. The author will show the vitality of Christian doctrines and their meaning for everyday life. Strong and fresh illustrations will hold the interest of the reader. At times the personal faith of the authors will be seen in illustrations from their own Christian pilgrimage.

Not all laymen are aware they are theologians. Many may believe they know nothing of theology. However, every person believes something. This series helps the layman to understand what he believes and to be able to be "prepared to make a defense to anyone who calls him to account for the hope that is in him" (1 Pet. 3:15, RSV).

To
my Colleagues of the faculty,
past and present,
of
New Orleans Baptist Theological Seminary

Preface

Readers will find this book more helpful if they know exactly what I set out to do and what I did not intend to do.

I did not intend to offer a defense of belief in God. This book is not apologetics. Its audience is neither the world in general nor intellectuals or other "cultured despisers" of religion in particular. This book is addressed to the community of faith, the church. It is written "from faith to faith" (Rom. 1:17).

I did not intend to offer a new understanding of God to the church. I believe that the traditional Christian understanding of God is correct. Of course, each generation of Christians must strive to appropriate that understanding for itself; I intend that this book would assist readers to do that.

I did not intend to offer devotional meditations about God. It is true that, as we internalize for ourselves the truth about God, this may move us deeply. But my purpose is not to move the readers, but to inform them.

I did intend, then, to explore the traditional Christian understanding of God responsibly and thoughtfully. The goal is to understand God better; this is one way of loving God with our minds (see Matt. 22:37).

In order to carry out this purpose, I have divided the book into three sections. In the first, I explore the divine self-relevation given in Jesus and the Bible. In the second, I provide a doctrinal portrait of God by speaking of His personhood and transcendence, His purpose, His activities, and His character. In the third section, I respond to three pressing questions concerning God: How do we believe in God in an age of unbelief? How can we believe in God in view of all the suffering in our world? How can God be both one and three?

I am aware of my indebtedness to many people. Where the debt is to authors and can be ascertained, I have given credit in the notes. I also am indebted to my secretary, Mrs. Anne Hanks, for her excellent typing. Much as I owe to others, the structure of the book and selection of its content are entirely mine, and for them I alone am responsible.

I am now in my fifteenth year of teaching at New Orleans Baptist Theological Seminary, a school to which I am deeply indebted. I take the liberty of dedicating this book to the faculty with whom I have served and continue to serve in that fine seminary.

Contents

Part I
Biblical

The Bible is about God. Yahweh, the God of Israel in the Old Testament, became flesh in Jesus Christ in the New Testament. The Bible may be read for its history, its poetry, or its wisdom; but it is understood properly only if one remembers that its real subject is God.

Since the Bible is a large book, it contains a great many insights concerning God. Everything which is affirmed in the Bible about God cannot be included here or, for that matter, in any other book. What is said here about God's self-relevation in the Bible is therefore selective; it is hoped that what has been selected is also in some sense representative of the biblical revelation of God.

I have just used the phrase "biblical revelation," which requires a brief word of explanation. I believe that the Bible is God's Word. The Bible was, of course, written by men, but in, with, and through their words is, I believe, the Word of God. As the titles of the first and third chapters in this part 1 indicate, the Bible will be treated herein as a divine self-revelation.

1
The Old Testament Revelation of God

The Story of Israel

The people who gave us the Bible were the Hebrews. Their story begins with God's call to Abraham to leave Ur of the Chaldees and to go to a new Promised Land. It continues through the adventures of the patriarchs—Isaac, Jacob, and Jacob's twelve sons. It arrives at a low point during the centuries of slavery in Egypt and then at a high point in God's mighty liberation of the people at the Exodus, under the leadership of Moses. Following the wilderness wanderings, the people finally inherited their Promised Land, led first by Joshua and then by the judges.

The center of the life of Israel was its covenant relationship with Yahweh, who said: "I . . . will be your God, and ye shall be my people" (Lev. 26:12). But under Saul, David, Solomon, and their successors, the people also found the kingship a unifying factor. During both the united monarchy and the divided kingdoms, God sent prophets to give His oracles to the people, calling them away from other gods to the true God. Throughout the history of Israel, the worship and moral life of Israel were guided by the Torah, the law of the Lord. The prophets warned Israel of the danger of religious rituals when they are practiced by people who are morally disobedient.

In 722 BC the city of Samaria fell to the Assryians, and the Northern Kingdom of Israel ceased to be an independent state. In 586 BC the Holy City, Jerusalem, fell to the Babylonians, and the Southern

Kingdom of Judah ceased to be an independent state. For all practical purposes, no independent Jewish nation existed from 586 BC until the founding of modern Israel in 1948. The loss of national independence in the sixth century before Christ was perhaps the greatest crisis in the history of the people of Israel. At that time, the element of hope entered into the national consciousness in a new way. Prophets gave God's promise to the people that some day He would establish a *shalom*, a new peace, a new prosperity. One example of this was given by Jeremiah:

> Behold, the days come, saith the Lord, that I will make a new covenant with the house of Israel, and with the house of Judah: Not according to the covenant that I made with their fathers in the day that I took them by the hand to bring them out of the land of Egypt; which my covenant they brake, although I was an husband unto them, saith the Lord: But this shall be the covenant that I will make with the house of Israel; After those days, saith the Lord, I will put my law in their inward parts, and write it in their hearts; and will be their God, and they shall be my people. And they shall teach no more every man his neighbour, and every man his brother, saying, Know the Lord: for they shall all know me, from the least of them unto the greatest of them. saith the Lord: for I will forgive their iniquity, and I will remember their sin no more (Jer. 31:31-34).

Clearly the central factor in Israel's life was its faith in Yahweh. This is not to say that Israel was always as faithful as she should have been. On the contrary. But it is to say that what characterizes these remarkable people, from their beginnings in Abraham to the time of Christ and indeed down to today, is their relationship to God. Kings, Temples, forms of worship, culture, prophets, and priests come and go in the life of these very durable people, but always one reality is constant: their God.

How might we characterize the God of Israel?

The Religiousness of Ancient Peoples

We begin our characterization of Israel's God by noting that ancient Israel shared in the general religious outlook of her neighbors in the ancient world. It is difficult for modern people to realize this, but all ancient people, so far as we can tell, were religious.

There were no atheists in the ancient world. Secularism was unknown. No one denied the reality of God. Religion was a universal fact. The outlook of all people was what we today would call supernatural, though ancient people did not have or need such a term.

Everyone believed that, in addition to the visible world, there is an unseen world of spiritual reality. Ancient people found this belief quite natural; as we would say today, they were socially conditioned to believe in gods (or God).

Thus the Old Testament contains no defense of the reality of God, no proofs for God's existence. It opens with the magnificent words, "In the beginning God." But it does not attempt to support the view that God was in the beginning. No support was required.

So Israel shared its religious outlook on life with other ancient people. But that does not mean that Israel's faith was in no way distinctive. On the contrary, Israel held a distinct understanding of God.

God Revealed Himself to Israel

Israel's distinctive understanding of God is to be attributed to the fact that Israel believed that God had revealed Himself to Israel. No one in Israel spoke about man proving God's existence or about man discovering God with his unaided mind or heart. Rather, Israel was convinced that God had manifested Himself. Israel's knowledge of the Lord rested on God's self-disclosure.

Of course, other ancient people felt that their gods also revealed themselves. So Israel was not unique in believing in revelation; she was, however, unique in believing the particular revelation which God gave to her. In other words, what was unique in her understanding of God was due to the fact that she had received her own particular revelation from her particular God, Yahweh.

Perhaps the point would be clearer if we contrasted Israel's position with that of her contemporaries and with that of some modern people.

Israel believed in the revelation which Yahweh had made to her;

she denied the revelation which was claimed by other nations for their gods. Other ancient nations, however, were more open-minded. They felt that their gods were revealed to them, but they did not deny that Israel's God was revealed to Israel. In other words, Israel's faith was more exclusive than that of her neighbors.

It was also more exclusive than that of some world religions today. Many Hindus, for example, are proud of their openness to other religions. They believe in their gods (sometimes said to number in the millions), but they do not reject the reality of other gods. This position is entirely unlike that of ancient Israel.

Also unlike the position of ancient Israel is the view that God may exist but if so He has not revealed Himself. Many modern, secular people are willing to admit that there may be a God; what they are very reluctant to admit is that God has truly disclosed Himself to anyone. The faith of ancient Israel was contrary to this. It rested on the conviction that God had revealed Himself to Israel.

The Varities of God's Self-Revelation

Israel believed that Yahweh is free. Among His freedoms is the freedom to reveal Himself by any means He may choose. The Old Testament records an astonishing variety of forms of God's self-revelation.

Several have already been mentioned. God revealed Himself by mighty acts in history, such as the Exodus; He revealed Himself in the Torah, the law; He revealed Himself through oracles delivered by prophets.

Many others might be mentioned. God revealed Himself through dreams (Gen. 41:25), through nature (Ps. 19:1), through miracles (Ex. 7—12), through writings (Jer. 30:1-2), and in other forms.

One means by which God revealed Himself, which many people find expecially illuminating, was through the religious experiences of some of Israel's leaders. For example, Moses heard the voice of the Lord speak to him out of a bush burning in the desert (Ex. 3:2). Isaiah was in the Temple in Jerusalem when he "saw the Lord . . . high and lifted up, and his train filled the temple" (Isa. 6:1). God called both these men to become His servants; then, with them as His spokemen, God revealed Himself to large numbers of people.

The variety of ways in which God revealed Himself in the Old Testament is a wonderful testimony to God's willingness to use many means in order to communicate with His people. But along with the variety of means of revelation, there was a uniform purpose. It was that the people come to know God and His purpose, activities, and character. This is a very important fact about God. He is willing to be known. Indeed, He acts to make Himself known to His people. This fact in itself tells us something very vital about God. He is not coy, not totally mysterious or totally hidden. He is a God who shows Himself to His people.

Of course, this does not mean that God reveals everything about Himself or that no mystery remains. The opposite is true. The more God reveals Himself to His people, the more mysterious He becomes. No one in the Old Testament claimed to know all about God. The people knew Him truly, but partially.

One way this is expressed in the Old Testament is that God is said to be heard but never to be seen. The word of the Lord was heard hundreds of times in Israel, in a variety of forms; but the Lord Himself did not appear to the eyes of men. He was concealed in a fiery pillar or cloud or in the smoke that filled the holy of holies on the Day of Atonement.

God could be heard but not seen; He revealed Himself really and truly, but never fully. The mystery of God remains in the midst of His self-revelation.

The Old Testament as a Book

We have been speaking of God's self-relevation in events and experiences which are recorded in the Hebrew Scriptures or, as we call it, the Old Testament. This means that the Old Testament contains accounts—a great many accounts—of revelations which God gave to His people at various times, in various ways.

But there is more to the Old Testament than that. For we believe that in addition to its being a record of divine self-revelations, the Old

Testament also is itself the Word of God. That is, it is a divine self-revelation.

What this means, in practical terms, is that as we read the Old Testament we should be attentive to the voice of God. We should read it not only in order to learn how God long ago revealed Himself to our spiritual ancestors but also so that God may reveal Himself to us today. When we read the Old Testament with a willingness to hear God's word, we will hear it.

Other ways of reading the Old Testament are ultimately unsatisfying. The Old Testament is about Yahweh, God who reveals Himself. To read the Old Testament without an openness to God's self-revelation in it is not consistent with the portrait of God which the Old Testament itself provides.

Israel's Growing Understanding of God

One of the advantages of believing the Old Testament to be the Word of God is that it puts us in a position to treat the Old Testament as a single book and to observe the development of Israel's understanding of God.

God did not give all of His revelation at any single time. Over many years, God continued to reveal more and more of Himself to His people as they were able to receive the revelation. God accommodated Himself to Israel's situation, and He enriched Israel's understanding as the situation developed.

Now I want you to give your attention to four developments in Israel's understanding of God. My concern is not to determine exactly when a particular idea, image, or concept of God, came to be accepted. Rather, I am concerned with the direction of Israel's thought. In other words, I am interested in the development rather than the date of an idea.

Polytheism, Henotheism, and Monotheism

Israel's understanding of God moved through a mixture of ideas of polytheism, henotheism, and monotheism. Let me explain what each of these words means.

Polytheism is belief in many gods. Many religions are polytheistic. Persons may be quite devoted to one god, their god, while believing that many other gods are equally real, powerful, and so on. Or, they may be devoted to several gods at once.

Israel's neighbors were polytheistic. There is one especially interesting story about this in 2 Kings 17:24-33. After Jerusalem had fallen in the sixth century, some foreigners were brought to settle in Israel. There they encountered difficulties, which they assumed were caused by their not knowing "the manner of the God of the land." Their assumption was that there are many gods (goddesses), each with his (her) own territory, and people moving into a new area should learn to get along with the god of that area.

Henotheism is the belief that there are many gods, but one is the supreme god and should be worshiped. Belief in one god supreme over all others is logically an interim position between polytheism and monotheism. Whether people are actually led to move toward monotheism by being attracted to henotheism is a different and difficult question.

Monotheism is the belief that there is only one true God. All other alleged gods are false, or idols.

The Bible begins with a clear affirmation of monotheism, but shows how polytheism resulted from human sin. The Hebrew people thus began their existence in a polytheistic city, Ur of the Chaldees. They encountered polytheism again in Egypt and again when they began to inherit the Promised Land. Perhaps they continued to encounter it throughout the Old Testament age, for the Assyrians and Babylonians who conquered Israel were polytheists.

There are some hints that Israel moved through a stage of henotheism. That is, some of the Israelites believed in Yahweh as the supreme God, but accepted the reality of the gods of other nations.

Of course, in a sense there were other gods. That is, there were objects of stone, metal, or wood; and those objects were real, and they were worshiped by Israel's neighbors. But, of course, they were not real gods. They were idols.

From Israel's montheistic point of view, "God" is a name, not a category. There is one and only one true God. From the point of view of polytheism or henotheism, "god" is a category. There are many gods with many names.

The shift from polytheism to monotheism took place over a long period of time. It probably had to be achieved over and over again, as the prophets and other leaders urged Israel to renounce all idols and to be loyal only to Yahweh.

Israel was the only monotheistic nation in the ancient world. This was in many ways its most distinctive feature. Students of ancient history who attempt to describe the contributions of various peoples are not likely to speak of Israel's art or form of government or mode of warfare or seagoing adventures; Israel's great contribution to civilization was monotheism.

But, of course, that is not how Israel would view it at all. They did not think of themselves as clever originators of a new idea. Rather, they thought of Yahweh as having revealed Himself to them. They were simply responding to the self-revelation of the true God.

Perhaps the most famous text concerning monotheism in the Old Testament is the one which goes by the name *Shema* which is its first word in Hebrew: "Hear, O Israel, the Lord our God is one Lord" (Deut. 6:4). Many other passages refer directly to monotheism, of course. Some of the most beautiful are found in Isaiah. For example, in Isaiah 40 we read:

> Hast thou not known? hast thou not heard, that the everlasting God, the Lord, the Creator of the ends of the earth, fainteth not, neither is weary? there is no searching of his understanding. He giveth power to the faint; and to them that have no might he increaseth strength. Even the youths shall faint and be weary, and the young men shall utterly fall· But they that wait upon the Lord shall renew their strength; they shall mount up with wings as eagles; they shall run, and not be weary; and they shall walk, and not faint (vv. 28-31).

The Rejection of Idols

As the people of Israel became more fully aware of God's revelation that He was the only true God, they had to face more directly the question of the status of the gods of their neighbors. It is not clear whether they did this quickly or over a long period of time. But eventually they arrived at the belief that the gods of their neighbors were not gods at all. They had no divine status. They were idols. They were without life or understanding or power. They were nothing but rocks or metal carved by men's hands.

Sometimes Israel seemed to take the idols quite seriously. For example, when any Israelite worshiped an idol, this was considered a serious betrayal of Yahweh. Some of the prophets likened it to marital infidelity (see Hos. 1:2).

But at other times Israel, recognizing that idols are mere stones or metal, nothing more, simply ridiculed idols and their worshipers. One example of this is found in Psalm 115:2-8:

> Wherefore should the heathen say, Where is now their God? But our God is in the heavens: he hath done whatsoever he hath pleased. Their idols are silver and gold, the work of men's hands. They have mouths, but they speak not: eyes have they, but they see not: They have ears, but they hear not: noses have they, but they smell not: They have hands, but they handle not: feet have they, but they walk not: neither speak they through their throat. They that make them are like unto them; so is every one that trusteth in them.

We today may tend to imagine that the worship of physical objects was very primitive and unsophisticated. Perhaps it was. But it is possible that idolaters felt that the stone images were only representations of their gods, which they believed to be more spiritual. Scholars debate about that.

Further, we may ask whether idolatry is entirely a matter of the past. If your "god" is whatever you prize, love, and honor above all else, then there is a great deal of idolatry in developed countries today. For many of our contemporaries are more committed to success, health, beauty, fame, comfort, knowledge, or power than to the true

God. We should not dismiss idolatry too quickly as a dead issue, since subtle forms of it persist in our own time.

God the Creator

Closely related to monotheism is the biblical teaching that God is the Creator of the world. This teaching could be called the success story of Jewish-Christian theology, for the vast majority of people in the Western world today assume that God is the Creator.

But the success of this idea should not conceal from us that it is by no means a self-evident idea; it was given by revelation. Many other ideas about the relationship between God and the world were held in the ancient world. For example, Plato believed that the world is uncreated and eternal, just as God is. The Stoics believed that the world is God's body, that God is, so to speak, the soul of the world. Many Gnostics believed that the world came out from God as rays of light come out from the sun. These views show the need for the revelation that God is the Creator.

What is being said is that the relationship between God and the world is somehow similar to the relationship between a human being and something which she or he creates.

In the Bible, a number of kinds of creative work are used to represent God's creative work. Consider this passage from Isaiah:

> Drop down, ye heavens, from above, and let the skies pour down righteousness: let the earth open, and let them bring forth salvation, and let righteousness spring up together; I the Lord have created it. Woe unto him that striveth with his Maker! Let the potsherd strive with the potsherds of the earth. Shall the clay say to him that fashioneth it, What makest thou? or thy work, He hath no hands? Woe unto him that saith unto his father, What begettest thou? or to the woman, What hast thou brought forth? Thus saith the Lord, the Holy One of Israel, and his Maker, Ask me of things to come . . . concerning the work of my hands command ye me. I have made the earth, and created man upon it: I, even my hands, have stretched out the heavens, and all their host have I commanded (45:8-12).

Here three different human creative acts are used to picture God's creative work. First, God created the world in something like the way a potter makes a piece of pottery. Second, God created the world in something like the way in which a man fathers a child or a mother gives birth to a child. Third, God created the world in something like the way in which a nomad puts up his tent. With these striking pictures, we learn about the creative work of God.

The most famous picture of God's creative work is found in Genesis 1. There God created by speaking. "And God said, Let there be light" (v. 3; see also v. 6,9,14,20,24). The picture here is of an Oriental monarch who gives a command and it is carried out. A king makes a war by ordering his generals to fight; he makes a city by ordering his builders to work. God created the world by speaking his orders that it be done, and it was done.

The idea that God is Creator is a very important one, and it influences us perhaps more that we realize. But as the various pictures of creation have been sketched out, you may have been wondering if they are adequate. Is God's creative work exactly like that of a potter making pottery or a woman giving birth to a child?

The answer, of course, is that God's creative work is not exactly like any human creative activity. God's creative work is somewhat like human creative work, but not exactly like it. And the Bible has an interesting way of expressing the uniqueness of God's creative work. It uses a Hebrew word, *bara,* for God's creative work and never uses that word for human creative work.

Since the close of the Old Testament, other ways of suggesting the uniqueness of God's creative work have been employed. The best known is to refer to God's creation as *creatio ex nihilo,* a Latin phrase meaning "creation out of nothing." This precise phrase does not appear in the Old Testament (though the idea is believed to be present in Genesis 1 and elsewhere). It was first used in a Latin translation of a Jewish book called 2 Maccabees, where we read: "I beg you, child, look at the sky and the earth; see all that is in them and realize that God made them out of nothing [Latin, *ex nihilo*], and that man comes into being in the same way" (2 Macc. 7:28, NEB). In the New Testament, we also find phrases which are very close to this, such as Paul's affimation that God "calleth into being the things that are not" (Rom. 4:17, author's translation).

No human creator can make something out of nothing. That is unique to God's creative activity. But some human creative activities seem to come closer than others to being creation out of nothing. Among modern creative activities, we think of the work of a composer and of the work of a novelist. These might help people today to understand God's creative work, for they are somewhat closer to creation out of nothing than, for example, a bricklayer who must have bricks and mortar in order to make a wall. What a novelist uses is not as tangible as bricks and mortar. He uses a language which he did not create and experiences from his past and his observations of people and things. But all of this is put together into a novel, not by the straightforward exercise of a skill but rather by a tremendous, energetic creativity.

We have been saying that the idea of God as Creator has a special meaning for Israel because of her monotheism. And these two teachings, so clearly expressed in the Old Testament, are filled with further implications about God. Four will be mentioned briefly. First, since God is Creator, He is personal. He is someone, not something. Things do not create; persons do.

Second, since God is Creator, He is utterly distinct from the world. We would never confuse a novelist with the book he wrote; we must never confuse God with the world He created.

Third, since God is the Creator of all the universe, He clearly is very wise and very powerful. As Creator He could never have made space and time, stars and galaxies, oceans and mountains, hummingbirds and roses, unless He had enormous power and knowledge.

Fourth, since God is Creator, there must be a purpose for the universe. Things are not all accidental, nor all unpredictable; God made the world for some reason. It would be very helpful for us, as we live our lives, to know what God's intention was in creating us. To know His purpose would be to know the true meaning of life.

Nature and History

A creator reveals something of himself in what he creates. For example, you can tell something about a novelist by reading his books. Similarly, you can tell something about God by looking at the world He has made. "The heavens declare the glory of God," wrote the psalmist, "and the firmament showeth his handiwork" (Ps. 19:1).

The people of Israel believed that God was active in nature. Thus, for example, they worshiped God at festivals which coincided with harvesttime because they believed that God gave them the harvest. Harvest festivals are found not only in Israel's religion but also in the religions of her neighbors.

However, Israel also had another kind of festival which none of her neighbors shared. It was a history festival. That is, it was a worship service which commemorated, not an event in nature, but an event in history.

One great example of this was Israel's Passover celebration. In it the people remembered the mighty deliverance which God provided to bring His people out of slavery in Egypt to freedom and a land of their own. Some Old Testament scholars regard Israel's conviction that God acted in history as well as in nature as one of the most distinctive beliefs in Israel. A good example of this was the American Old Testament scholar, G. Ernest Wright, who argued in his book *God Who Acts* that Israel's theology was not a product of abstract reasoning, but rather a faithful remembering and reciting of the mighty acts of God in her history.

Of course, revelation through history is not an exhaustive description of the Old Testament revelation. For example, Proverbs is a distillation of Israel's wisdom about how life is to be lived, and in it God's mighty acts in history do not play a large role. But in much of the Old Testament the idea of God's historical acts is central, and Wright was correct to say that this was characteristic of Israel's theology.

Psalm 105 provides a good example of the way in which Israel's theology was a recital of God's mighty acts and how her worship was a celebration of God's mighty acts. It opens by urging the people to worship and thank God for his mighty deeds: "O Give thanks unto the Lord; call upon his name: make known his deeds among the people. Sing unto him, sing psalms unto him: talk ye of all his wondrous works" (vv. 1-2). It continues by reciting His covenant with Abraham, Isaac, and Jacob (vv. 8-11). It goes on to speak of the rescue from Egypt (vv. 26-27) and of Israel's wilderness experience and finally inheriting the land (vv. 38-45).

God's self-revelation is closely tied up with His acts in history. Though He revealed Himself in various ways, the revelation given in the mighty acts was a central one for Israel.

What was revealed about God by mighty acts, such as the deliverance from Egypt? These acts confirmed that God had selected Israel to be His own; they were an elect people, a Chosen People. The acts also confirmed that God had bound Israel to Himself by a covenant, the central idea of the covenant being found in the words, "I . . . will be your God, and ye shall be my people" (Lev. 26:12). One early expression of all these ideas—election, covenant, and mighty acts—is found in Deuteronomy:

> The Lord did not set his love upon you, nor choose you, because ye were more in number than any people; for ye were the fewest of all people: But because the Lord loved you, and because he would keep the oath which he had sworn unto your fathers, hath the Lord brought you out with a mighty hand, and redeemed you out of the house of bondmen, from the hand of Pharaoh king of Egypt. Know therefore that the Lord thy God, he is God, the faithful God, which keepeth covenant and mercy with them that love him and keep his commandments to a thousand generations (7:7-9).

One consequence of Israel's belief that God acted in history to save His people is that the faith of Israel was badly shaken when God failed to deliver His people. The fall of Samaria and later of Jerusalem were spiritual as well as political crises. How could Israel continue to believe after the fall of Jerusalem that God acts in history to save His people?

They did so by turning their eyes from the past to the future. They began to hope for a new deliverance, a new act of God to save. Prophets from Jeremiah onward began to anticipate what that would be like. For example, Ezekiel, a prophet who was among those exiled to Babylon, expressed the promise of the Lord as follows:

> Therefore say, Thus saith the Lord God; Although I have cast them far off among the heathen, . . . yet will I be to them as a little sanctuary in the countries where they shall come. Therefore say, Thus saith the Lord God; I will even gather you from the people, and assemble you out of the countries where ye have been scattered, and I will give you the land of Israel. And they shall come thither, and they shall take away all the detestable things thereof and all the abominations thereof from thence. And I will give them one heart, and I will put a new spirit within you; and I will take the stony heart out of their flesh, and will give them an heart of flesh: That they may walk in my statues, and keep mine ordinances, and do them: and they shall be my people, and I will be their God (11:16-20).

He foresaw the people in their own land again, at peace, worshiping the Lord alone, obeying His law, and with new hearts filled with loyalty and obedience toward the Lord rather than with stubbornness and disobedience.

The promise of God concerning the future was given by many prophets. Hope became an important aspect of the religious faith of Israel.

Ritualism and Morality

Another implication of election-covenant-mighty-acts was that Israel was obligated to live according to the Torah or law of God. This is evident in the passages which speak of God's mighty acts. Thus Psalm 105:45 says that God made Israel a nation "that they might observe his statues, and keep his laws." And Deuteronomy 7:9 reports that the Lord kept covenant with "them that love him and keep his commandments."

The part of the Torah which most of us remember best is the Ten Commandments (Ex. 20; Deut. 5). These include commands about relating properly to God (the first four) and to fellow Israelites (the other six). We today might describe these groups as religious and moral commands.

But the Torah contains many other commands in addition to these ten. It contains commands about avoiding unclean foods, about the punishment of crimes, about how the worship of God should be conducted, and about sacrifices and other worship rituals.

In the Torah, the commands about rituals and the commands about moral matters are not separated; they are all mixed up. All were commanded by the Lord, so all would have appeared to Israel as equally important.

And that is where the problems arose, for it was easy for the people to slip into ritualism and ignore the moral commands. That is, they often ignored the moral commands but carefully observed the sacrifices which the Lord had provided for the cleansing of sins. This meant, for example, that a powerful man could steal a defenseless widow's land and add it to his own, then use her as a servant, and then offer a large sin offering to cover his sin. This kind of practice occurred frequently in Israel during the time of the divided kingdom.

And so God sent messengers to denounce it. One of the earliest was Amos, and his denunciation of ritualism was scathing. He described the evil practices of the powerful as follows:

> They hate him that rebuketh in the gate, and they abhor him that speaketh uprightly. Forasmuch therefore as your treading is upon the poor, and ye take from him burdens of wheat: ye have built houses of hewn stone, but ye shall not dwell in them; ye have planted pleasant vineyards, but ye shall not drink wine of them. For I know your manifold transgressions and your mighty sins: they afflict the just, they take a bribe, and they turn aside the poor in the gate from their right (Amos 5:10-12).

Then he expressed God's feelings about the "worship" of such evil people:

> I hate, I despise your feast days, and I will not smell in your solemn assemblies. Though ye offer me burnt offerings, . . . I will not accept

them: neither will I regard the peace offerings of your fat beasts. Take thou away from me the noise of thy songs; for I will not hear the melody of thy viols. But let judgment run down as waters, and righteousness as a mighty stream (vv. 21-24).

Amos and other prophets of the eighth and seventh centuries before Christ helped Israel to make a third movement, from ritualism to morality. They did not say that the commands about worship rituals in the Torah were wrong. But they did insist that keeping worship rituals alone is not a sufficient religious response to the Lord. God is more concerned about justice and righteousness, about compassion and truth, than He is about rituals, even if He Himself did command that the rituals be observed.

Doubtless this lesson, like the lessons concerning monotheism and history, had to be learned over and over by Israel. But the message of prophets like Amos was written down, and it is so clear that we today can easily understand it: God is more concerned about moral goodness than about rituals.

This tells us something about how persons should respond to God. But it also tells us something about God. It tells us that moral goodness is a priority with Him. And the moment we ask why this is so, we know the answer: It is because He Himself is a righteous God. That is, He is faithful to his word; He expects people to act in the same way. He honors His covenant with Israel; He expects Israel to honor the covenant too. He is compassionate toward the weak, and He expects His people to be compassionate also.

This is a very important revelation of God. To know that God is a God of goodness is one of the most important things we can know about God. It means that He is for what is good in our world and against the evil. It means that He is not arbitrary or unpredictable or vindictive. It means that He will do what is right and noble and good. It means, in short, that God may be trusted.

Nationalism and Universalism

I have spoken of three movements in Israel's understanding of God: from polytheism to monotheism, from nature to history, and from ritualism to morality. Now we will observe a fourth movement, from nationalism to universalism.

It is not difficult to understand how Israel came to hold a nationalistic view of God. After all, God had chosen Israel to be His people; He had entered into a covenant with Israel alone; He had given His Torah to Israel alone; He had delivered Israel by His mighty acts. It must have been easy for Israel to assume that God was not really concerned about other nations.

But from the beginning, God had been revealing that His concern reached to all nations and people. He had said to Abraham, "I will bless thee," and to this He had added, ". . . and in thee shall all families of the earth be blessed" (Gen. 12:2-3). Abraham's descendants were clear about the first part, but it took them a long time to grasp the second.

Perhaps the most famous Old Testament story about an Israelite being led to make the move from nationalism to universalism is the story of Jonah. Jonah was commanded to go to a non-Jewish city, Nineveh, to preach. Rather than preach to non-Israelites, he ran away from Nineveh. When the Lord finally coerced the prophet to go to Nineveh, the city repented. And Jonah was furious! He resented God's being gracious and compassionate toward anyone other than Israel (see Jonah 1:1-3; 4:1-2).

But eventually many in Israel came to accept the idea that the Lord is concerned about all human beings, not merely about national Israel. Doubtless this lesson had to be learned over and over again, as the earlier three did. But it was learned, and that marked an important point in Israel's understanding of God.

A Summary

We have been examining some representative ideas about God as He revealed himself to Israel and as He reveals Himself to us as we study the Old Testament. Now I want to try to summarize some of this revelation in a few words.

There is one ultimate reality—a personal God who exists independently of our world and who created our world and now is Lord of it, both of nature and of human history. He entered into a covenant relationship with Abraham and his descendants, and He repeatedly acted in history to ensure their continuance as His people. He formed them into a community and demanded moral obedience of them, gradually leading them on to a more profound understanding of Himself and of His purpose. The Old Testament closes with God's work incomplete and with the people hoping for a more complete implementation of the divine purpose. In all of this—creation, election, covenant, law, prophets, wisdom, hope—God is understood to be gracious, kind, forgiving, and loving, as well as righteous, powerful, and wise.

2

Jesus' Revelation of God

The Story of Jesus

Jesus is probably the most widely known person who ever lived on earth. Hundreds of millions of people have been and are familiar with His life and work.

When Augustus Caesar ruled the Roman Empire, Jesus was born in the land called Judah, in a village named Bethlehem, in an animal shed, and His mother Mary and her husband Joseph wrapped Him up and laid Him in a feed trough. He grew up in a town in Galilee called Nazareth. At about the age of thirty, He received baptism at the hands of the prophet John the Baptist, and Jesus' public work began. It was to be a brief ministry of about three years, and yet it would change forever the course of human history. Jesus' work consisted principally of calling a group of followers, of preaching and teaching, and of healing sick and injured people who came to Him for help.

Jesus' preaching antagonized some Jewish leaders, who took steps to have Him silenced. In what is almost universally condemned as an outrage, they contrived to have the Roman procurator, Pontius Pilate, put Jesus to death. He was crucified when Tiberius was the emperor of Rome. As we all know, that was not the end of His story. We shall talk about its sequel, the resurrection, in the next chapter.

A New Revelation

An early unknown Christian began a letter to some fellow Christians with these words: "God, who at sundry times and in divers manners spake in time past unto the fathers by the prophets, Hath in these last days spoken unto us by his Son" (Heb. 1:1-2). What the writer was saying is that, as wonderful as the self-revelation of God to Israel was, the self-revelation which God gave in Jesus is more wonderful still. All Christians would surely agree that Jesus' revelation of God is greater than the revelation given in the Old Testament. But before we rush on to say how it was, let us notice what an astonishing thing is being said.

For more than a dozen centuries, God had worked with His people Israel to help them know Him. He had used numerous methods to reveal to them His character and purpose. He had corrected their mistakes and taken them progressively deeper into the truth about Himself. This unfolding self-revelation continued for hundreds of years in the lives of thousands of people.

Then in three brief years, in the life of a single person, God revealed Himself in a way that surpassed all that He had done before! It is truly an amazing thing. And yet, as we all recognize, it is surely the case.

Image and Word

Various writers refer to Jesus' revelation of God. We have mentioned the author of Hebrews. We will now consider briefly two other writers, Paul and John.

In his Letter to the Colossians, Paul referred to Jesus as "the image of the invisible God" (1:15). It is such a familiar phrase that it is easy to miss its significance.

God is invisible. He cannot be seen by human eyes. Further, God commands that no image of Him be made (Ex. 20:4-6). Yet He wants to reveal Himself fully to humanity. And so He gave to mankind an image of Himself, so that we may see what He is like. That image is not made of stone or metal, but of flesh and bone. It is not a carved statue, but a living Person. When you look at Jesus of Nazareth, you "see" God, for He is the image of God.

Perhaps Paul was thinking of a saying of Jesus which is recorded for us in the Gospel of John. One of Jesus' disciples asked Jesus, "Shew us the Father." Jesus replied, "He that hath seen me hath seen the Father" (John 14:8-9).

John himself had hinted that Jesus is the visible image of the invisible God, when he wrote: "No man hath seen God at any time. The only begotten Son, which is in the bosom of the Father, he hath declared him" (John 1:18).

That saying is from the prologue to John's Gospel, which is famous for another way of expressing Jesus' revelation of God. John began with words which sound very much like the opening words of Genesis, but with a new twist. "In the beginning," he wrote, "was the Word" (1:1). It was by His word that God created the world (see Gen. 1:3,6,9,14,20,24), and it was the word of God which came to Israel by the prophets when they announced, "Thus saith the Lord."

But John was thinking of a new coming of God's Word, as we see from this sentence: "And the word was made flesh, and dwelt among us." God's Word became a flesh-and-blood human being named Jesus. God's Word was, as we say, incarnated in one historical man. "(And we beheld his glory, glory as of the only begotten . . . ,) full of grace and truth" (John 1:14). Jesus was the enfleshment of the Word of God. God's glory shown out of His life. And the Word of God was full of grace and truth (reality).

God has spoken to us by His Son Jesus. Jesus is the visible image of the invisible God. Jesus is the Word of God incarnate.

These are truths which all Christians believe deeply, for we have come to know God, to believe in Him, precisely through the great revelation which He gave of Himself in Jesus. Of course, we may know about God from nature or conscience or some other source, but for us the ultimate and definitive revelation of God is Jesus. That is why we are Christians.

An Indirect Revelation

Now let us consider how Jesus went about revealing God. Our initial reaction to this suggestion may be to think that it is a waste of time. We might think that the answer is obvious: Jesus revealed God by talking about Him.

But it is not quite that simple. For one thing, Jesus was not a professor of theology! He did not give a series of lectures about God, nor did He write a book about God. He did not say, "I want to tell you about God," nor did He say, "I want to correct some misunderstandings about God."

His revelation of God was not given that directly. It was given indirectly in His preaching and teaching and even more indirectly in his other ministries and activities. We will now consider several aspects of Jesus' life and work in order to see what they tell us about God.

Jesus and the Jewish Religion

Jesus was a devout Jew. His life was one of devotion to the God of Abraham, Isaac, and Jacob. He believed in the Hebrew Scriptures and quoted them frequently.

As a devout Jew, he was deeply religious. He put God first. This is clear throughout Jesus' life. As early as age twelve, He could ask Mary and Joseph, "Wist ye not that I must be about my Father's business?" (Luke 2:49). In the Sermon on the Mount, He urged His followers, "Seek ye first the kingdom of God" (Matt. 6:33), and He could well have added, "even as I do."

We today are not accustomed to speaking of Jesus as a religious person. That is because we ourselves have religious faith in Jesus. In the following chapter, I shall attempt to say why it is correct to have religious faith in Jesus. But now we need to notice that, although it may seem contradictory, the One in whom we put our faith directed His faith and worship and prayers to the God of Israel. The Gospels are quite clear about this, and we should be also: Jesus was a devoutly religious Jewish man. Thus He confirmed that the Old Testament revelation of God was true and trustworthy.

The Kingdom of God

During the period of His public ministry, Jesus frequently preached, usually in Galilee, often out-of-doors, sometimes in synagogues. His sermons were full of stories (we call them parables) and brief, memorable sayings. They were easily recalled by His followers years after He had ascended, so they must have been very powerful sermons.

One of the four Gospels, Mark, contains records of many of Jesus' activities but not of much of His preaching and teaching. But early in the Gospel, Mark gave a brief statement which is apparently intended to be a summary of Jesus' preaching. These are Mark's words: "Now after that John was put in prison, Jesus came into Galilee, preaching the gospel of the kingdom of God, And saying, The time is fulfilled, and the kingdom of God is at hand: repent ye, and believe the gospel" (1:14-15).

If this is, as I believe, intended to summarize what Jesus usually said in His sermons, then clearly the central content of His preaching was the kingdom of God. That this was His central theme is confirmed by the fact that, when we examine His famous stories (or parables), we find that most of them are explicitly said to be about the kingdom of God.

What did Jesus mean by the kingdom of God? This is a controversial subject. I will attempt to offer general comments about it which would be acceptable to many scholars.[1]

The Old Testament does not contain the phrase "the kingdom of God," but the idea that God is King and that He rules over a kingdom appears in the Old Testament. For example, we are told in Psalm 103:19 that God rules in heaven.

Jesus taught that the most important thing in a person's life is for that person to gain the kingdom of God. The kingdom of God is like a pearl so precious that a person should sell everything he has in order to secure it (Matt. 13:44-46).

Jesus also taught that the kingdom of God looks unimpressive, but, in fact, it is going to grow into something tremendously large, like a tiny mustard seed that grows into a large bush which can shelter God's creatures (Mark 4:30-32).

By the kingdom of God, Jesus did not mean a geographical or a political entity. He did not identify it with the Promised Land or with the national state of Israel.

Jesus thought of the kingdom of God as an end-time reality. That is, it is something which God was doing to fulfill the hopes of Israel. It was a new act of God, inaugurating a new age in the relations between God and humanity.

In brief, the kingdom of God is God's sovereign rule. In the Lord's prayer, three phrases occur, one after another. "Hallowed be thy name. Thy kingdom come. Thy will be done on earth, as it is in heaven" (Matt. 6:9-10). They all mean just about the same thing. The first means: May you be revealed and honored and accepted as God. The second means: May your sovereign rule come to pass. The third means: May your purpose be carried out here. The will of God is for God's kingdom to come, and the kingdom of God has come whenever God is honored as God.

So, the central theme in Jesus' preaching was the fulfillment of a hope for the end-time, when God's rule would be extended over people's lives. The people of the kingdom are those who have accepted God's rule. They do not create or build the kingdom. Only God does that. All that human beings can do is to open their hearts to receive the rule of God and pray that it may come.

What did Jesus believe about when God's kingdom would come? That is a controverisal point. At times He seemed to say that it would come at some unspecified date in the future (for example, see Matt. 25:1 *ff*.). Therefore, we must assume that in one sense the kingdom was yet to come; perhaps in a sense it still is future.

But that is not the whole story. For Jesus also spoke of the kingdom as coming in His own time. In the summary given in Mark, Jesus said, "The time is fulfilled, and the kingdom of God is at hand" (1:15). Elsewhere He was even more explicit. Once when He was questioned about healing a dumb man, Jesus responded: "But if I with the finger of God cast out devils, no doubt the kingdom of God is come upon you" (Luke 11:20).

So in one sense the kingdom or end-time rule of God was a future event. But in another sense, it had arrived. It was present in Jesus Himself, as He did his ministry of healing. And when He preached, He urged His listeners to open their lives to God's rule.

We have twice referred to Jesus' inviting people to receive the kingdom. A word needs to be said about which people He invited. The answer is that He invited everyone. He did not confine His invitation to the wealthy, the powerful, the religious, the upright, or the socially accepted people of His day (in Jesus' day, wealth was considered by many to be a sign of God's blessing upon a good person). He invited everyone, without distinction. He spoke about God sending His servants out into the "highways and hedges" to find people to come into His kingdom for, He said, it is more difficult for a rich man to go into the kingdom than for a camel to go through the eye of a needle (Matt. 19:24). He said that the prostitutes and tax-collectors (lackeys of the hated Roman rulers) would go into the kingdom before more religious and moral people (Matt. 21:31). In short, Jesus offered the kingdom or rule of God to everyone equally, with the expectation that the social outcasts and failures were more likely to receive it than the religious, moral, powerful, and wealthy.

If we wanted to try to express in language familiar to the church today what Jesus was saying about the kingdom of God, we might put it like this. Jesus preached that in His own time, through Himself, God was performing a unique act of grace and salvation, and Jesus invited everyone without distinction to commit himself to God in order to receive this salvation.

Jesus' proclamation of the kingdom of God is built upon the Old Testament revelation of God. But it makes an enlargement and enrichment of that revelation. It tells of a new act of God heretofore hoped for but not realized. In short, Jesus brought a new revelation of God's purpose and work in His message about the kingdom.

The Priority of Love

In preaching about God's kingdom, Jesus was fulfilling His role of a prophet. He also fulfilled the role of a rabbi, or teacher.[2] He taught people about what we today would call moral issues. In the language of His times, He taught about Torah, the law of God.

He did this at various times, but one occasion has special importance for us. A listener, himself a teacher of the law, asked Jesus a question. He wanted to know which of the commandments was the most important. This was the ultimate question for a Jew to ask, for the commands are God's law; to ask about the most important commandment was to ask about the most important thing in life. We might express his question today with words such as, What is the meaning of life? or What is the most important thing in life?

Jesus clearly had thought about this matter carefully, and he answered without hesitation. First he quoted from Deuteronomy:

> The first of all the commandments is, Hear, O Israel; The Lord our God is one Lord: And thou shalt love the Lord thy God with all thy heart, and with all thy soul, and with all thy mind, and with all thy strength: this is the first commandment (Mark 12:29-30).

Then he added a second quotation from Leviticus. "And the second is like, namely this, Thou shalt love thy neighbor as thyself. There is none other commandment greater than these" (v. 31).

The simplicity of Jesus' statement is striking. Out of hundreds of commandments in the Torah, Jesus selected two. Both were about love, the first about love for God and the second about love for one's neighbor.

Jesus gave His questioner even more than he asked for. He not only gave the man the most important commandments but also told him that these two are a summary of all the commandments (Matt. 22:40). In other words, if you keep these two commands, you have kept all the law. "Love is the fulfilling of the law" (Rom. 13:10).

We might express this in a modern way by saying that the meaning of human life is love. The true destiny of every human being is to become a lover of God and a lover of other people.

This teaching of Jesus has enormous implications for His understanding of God. Just as God had revealed that He was more concerned about righteousness than about rituals through the prophetic message that empty ritualism was wrong, so God revealed that his nature is love through Jesus' teaching that love is the fulfillment of the law. Jesus did not often talk directly about God's love, but indirectly He spoke forcefully about God's love in giving the two great commands. And, of course, the love of God was assumed by Jesus when He invited into the kingdom sinners as well as righteous people; that was a clear indication of God's attitudes toward sinners.

The Father

We have seen that Jesus was utterly devoted to God as He was revealed in the Old Testament. He preached that, through Himself, God was extending His gracious rule into the lives of all kinds of people. He taught that love is the ultimate priority in human life, presumably because it is the ultimate characteristic of God's life.

There is one word which brings together these revelations of God. It is the word *Father.* Jesus used it over and over. In His prayers, He addressed God as *Abba,* an Aramaic word meaning "father" or "daddy."

The Old Testament contains a few scattered references to God's fatherhood. One of these is Psalm 103:13, "Like as a father pitieth his children, so the Lord pitieth them that fear him." The prophets occasionally spoke of Israel as God's child. But the fatherhood of God was not a major theme in the Old Testament.

It is not too much to say that Jesus selected this image of God out of many in the Old Testament and made it central to His understanding of God. Or we could put it the other way round and say that God revealed to Jesus that they were related to each other in a Father-Son relationship. At Jesus' baptism, Jesus heard God's voice say to Him, "Thou are my beloved Son"; He never forgot it (see Luke 3:22).

Not only did Jesus address God as *Abba* but He also told a story in which He Himself figured as the only Son of God (see Mark 12:1-8).

This was unique to Jesus. No earlier prophet had spoken of himself as a son of God, certainly not as the only Son of God. And no one before Jesus had dared to address God with the intimate term *Abba*.

But that is not all that we learn about God's fatherhood. For Jesus invited His followers to think of God as their Father too! He taught them to begin their prayers with the words, "Our Father" (Matt. 6:9). He referred to God as "your father" (v. 8). He said that God, like a father, gives gifts to His people (Matt. 7:11) and knows what they need (Luke 12:30). God forgives as a father forgives his prodigal son (Luke 15:11-24). Having experienced a uniquely close relationship with God, Jesus introduced His followers into the same relationship.

And yet, not exactly the same. For the New Testament contains careful distinctions between the unique sonship of Jesus and the sonship of all God's other children. For example, Jesus Himself spoke of "my father" and "your father" but not of "our father." Again, John expressed Jesus' unique sonship by referring to Jesus as the only-begotten (Greek, *monogenēs*) Son of God and of Jesus' followers as sons of God (see John 1:12,14). Further, Paul made the same distinction by saying that Jesus was God's firstborn (there can be only one firstborn) and Christians are God's adopted sons (see Rom. 8:15,29).

That God is a Father to human beings is now widely accepted, but that was not the case before Jesus came. He gave us the revelation of God as Father. It is an image of God which brings together in a powerful synthesis God's sovereign rule and His compassion for all people.

A Community

We saw that, in the Old Testament, God was concerned to create a people of His own and that He chose Israel and entered into a covenant with her which is summarized in the words, "I will be your God, and you shall be my people."

Jesus did not talk very directly about a people of God. He did, however, confirm indirectly that God is concerned to create a people, and He gave a new understanding of who those people would be.

Two themes of Jesus implied that God is concerned to create a people. One is the kingdom of God. The kingdom is not the people, of course; the kingdom is God's rule. But the rule of God implies a people, namely, those who have accepted the rule of God which is being extended through Jesus' work.

The other theme which implied that God is concerned to create a people was the theme of fatherhood. The moment that Jesus began to teach people to think of God as their Father, He began to imply that they were God's children. Jesus believed that God was creating a family for Himself.

But who was to be a part of God's people or family? According to Jesus, it was not the nation of Israel. Nor were God's people the morally upright or the socially acceptable. Rather, the people of God was a new community made up of those who heard Jesus' message and accepted His invitation into the kingdom.

Jesus did not exactly found a new religion in the way that Muhammad or Gautama Buddha did. He Himself never left the Jewish religion, nor did He suggest that His followers leave.

And yet, He did set in motion the creation of a new community, a new Israel, as it were. The new community could not be identified with any previous configuration of persons. It is open to all without distinction. The prerequisite for entering it is to have heard Jesus' message and accepted it.

One clue to Jesus' intention was His choice of twelve men to be especially close companions. The Gospels often refer to these men as the twelve (see, for example, Luke 6:12-16). In choosing exactly twelve men, Jesus was giving a symbol. As the nation of Israel had descended from the twelve sons of Jacob and had existed as twelve tribes, so Jesus' new community would have these twelve men as its nucleus.

Thus, Jesus confirmed the Old Testament teaching that God's purpose is to create a people for Himself. But He offered a new insight into who those people are. They are those who hear Jesus' message and accept it. God in His grace will receive anyone who comes, even those most disapproved of by society, even the unreligious and the immoral.

Jesus' invitation was not addressed so much to Israel as a nation as it was, and is, to individuals. Each person who heard Jesus' message had the opportunity to accept it. One by one, they could come into the kingdom.

Is this individualism? Yes and no. Yes, in the sense that each person must accept God's rule for himself; it cannot be done by one's nation or family. But no, in the sense that what one comes to as an individual is precisely a new community, the family of God. Whoever truly calls God "Father" has all the rest of God's children as his brothers and sisters.

Jesus in His Own Preaching

Now we must briefly consider one of the most unusual things about Jesus' message. Its full implications will not become clear until the next chapter of this book, but we need to recognize it at this point in our study.

It is this: Jesus preached about Himself.

Not entirely, of course. We have seen that His central theme was the kingdom of God. But Jesus included Himself in His message.

.This was an extraordinary thing to do. No Old Testament prophet had done it. Isaiah was not part of his own message, nor Jeremiah of his.

Yet Jesus was part of His own message. He spoke of Himself as God's only Son (Mark 12:1-8). He saw God's kingdom as coming uniquely in Himself. He called the twelve and others to be followers of Himself. He referred to Himself as the judge of mankind (Matt. 25:31-46).

What are we to make of this? Was Jesus a self-centered person? Not at all! Jesus clearly was a very humble person. He spoke about being a servant rather that about being served (Mark 10:45). He gave Himself unselfishly to help others, to heal them, to point them to God.

And yet, He clearly spoke also about Himself, even in connection with service. Perhaps the best example of this is His instituting the Lord's Supper (see Matt. 26:26-30). During Passover week, when good Jews remembered and celebrated God's deliverance of Israel from Egypt, Jesus told His followers to begin a new celebration—the remembering and celebrating of His death! By eating bread and drinking wine, they were to remember forever His death upon the cross, His broken body and shed blood.

Others had died for their faith in God—Isaiah, Jeremiah, and others. But they did not ask people to remember them. They pointed away from themselves, to God.

How did Jesus, an unselfish, humble, self-giving, servant of others, come to preach about Himself, call people to follow Him, and instruct them to remember His death?

It is clearly a mystery. The only possible answer is, of course, that somehow Jesus ought to have been part of His own message. In other words, there was something about Him, something we have not yet spoken of, which justified His being part of His own message.

But Jesus' disciples did not understand this during His time with them. And so we, like them, must wait to see the meaning of this extraordinary fact.

But, of course, Jesus' disciples did follow Him and accept His words about Himself, even though they did not understand this meaning. And they did so for a very good reason. Jesus performed deeds which validated that He was indeed a special person.

The Authority of Jesus

Mark's Gospel tells us that Jesus preached a sermon in the synagogue in His hometown, Nazareth, and afterward He healed several people. The response of those present is interesting: "And they were all amazed, insomuch that they questioned among themselves, saying, What thing is this? what new doctrine is this? for with authority commandeth he even the unclean spirits, and they do obey him" (Mark 1:27). Clearly Jesus had a special kind of authority.

This became clear in a number of ways during Jesus' ministry. In the Sermon on the Mount, Jesus seemed to equate His authority with that of the Torah (Matt. 5:17-48). He forgave sins, a perogative of God (Mark 2:1-12). By His miracles, He demonstrated authority over nature, so that His disciples exclaimed, "What manner of man is this, that even the winds and the sea obey him" (Matt. 8:27). He asserted

His authority over the sabbath (Matt. 12:1-14) and over Satan (Matt. 12:22-28) and over diseases (Matt. 9:1-8).

The authority of Jesus was asserted in words and validated by deeds. We can understand how Peter referred to Jesus as "a man approved of God among you by miracles and wonders and signs which God did by him in the midst of you, as ye yourselves also know" (Acts 2:22). In the exercise of His power and knowledge, Jesus demonstrated the appropriateness of making Himself a part of His own message. Clearly many people who heard him were forced to respond not only to His message but to Jesus Himself.

In the next chapter, we will learn more of the ultimate justification for Jesus' self-proclamation.

The Revelation of the Old Testament

We have seen that God revealed Himself to His people Israel, and that revelation is recorded in the Old Testament. God also revealed Himself in His Son, Jesus, a revelation recorded in the Gospels. What is the relationship between the revelation given in the Old Testament and the one given in Jesus?

Three things might be said. First, in some instances what Jesus provided was a selective representation of Old Testament themes. For example, Jesus selected the Old Testament teaching about God as Father and presented it with a new emphasis. He also selected two commands about love from the Torah and presented them as the fulfillment of all the law.

Second, Jesus enlarged and enriched some of the Old Testament revelation about God. The best example of this is the kingdom of God, a minor theme in the Old Testament but the central theme of Jesus' preaching. Jesus enriched it by saying that the kingdom was being extended into person's lives through His own work.

Third, Jesus offered a course correction, if not for the Old Testament itself, at least for the understanding of it which prevailed in the Judaism of His day. An outstanding example of this was Jesus' revelation that God cared just as much about society's outcasts and life's failures as about the religiously and morally upright.

When we consider how much Jesus revealed about God, His grace and salvation and purpose, we understand even better the superiority of Jesus' revelation to all that had come before Him (Heb. 1:1-2). As grateful as we may be for what God revealed to Israel, still we would be impoverished if that were all we knew of God: Jesus truly was the visible image of an otherwise invisible God.

Notes

1. In this section, I am indebted to an article by H. Joseph Blair entitled "The Kingdom of God in the Teaching of Jesus," found in *The Theological Educator* (Spring 1982, pp. 42 *ff*).

2. He was called both prophet and rabbi during His lifetime (see Matt. 21:11; John 3:2).

3
The New Testament Revelation of God

The Story of Easter

It would be difficult to imagine a more dispirited group of people than the followers of Jesus on the day after His death. They had thought that He was to redeem Israel; instead, He had died. And He died the death, not of an ordinary man, but a death appropriate to the worst criminals of society, crucified, indeed, between two such persons. What was the good of His power to heal others, if He could not save Himself (Matt. 27:42)? What was the use of His marvelous teachings, if He and they could be so quickly and completely silenced by Roman imperial power? Peter expressed the despair and resignation of them all when he stated that he intended to return to Galilee and begin fishing again (John 21:3).

But the next morning, the first Easter morning, everything was changed. God raised His Son from the dead. Jesus began to appear to various loyal followers—first to some women, then to some men, eventually to all the twelve (or eleven) at once. He was changed, so that they did not always recognize Him at once, but He was the same person they had known. When some of them went to Jesus' tomb, they found it empty. He traveled with two disciples and appeared to some in Jerusalem and to some in Galilee.

He did not appear to people who had faith. No one had faith. He appeared to those who had loved him; and by appearing, He gave them faith. They knew how incredible it was that a dead man should be alive again; but there He was, in front of them. They had no choice but to accept Him.

There is a mystery about what happened. No one was there to see it; they learned about it after it was done. They never fully understood it, nor do we today. Jesus was changed, clearly, yet He was the same person as before. The mystery remains.

But so does the fact. Something happened, happened in the life of Jesus and in the lives of the disciples, something which transformed them from people of despair to people of hope and faith and courage. And the change in them was mediated through them to everyone who believed their story. The result was the birth of the Christian church and the transformation of human history.

The name which they gave to the mysterious event was *resurrection.*

The Meaning of Christ's Resurrection

Three questions could be asked concerning the resurrection of Christ. First, what is the evidence for it? This is an important question, and I believe that the evidence for it is quite good.[1] But we will not be discussing that question here. We will take for granted that Christ was raised.

A second question is, What did the resurrection of Christ symbolize? In other words, to what did it point, beyond itself? This too is an important question. But we will not spend our time here with it.

Our concern is for another question, namely, What is the meaning of the resurrection of Christ? What exactly is its religious importance and signification?

Four things may be said.

First, the resurrection means that Jesus is alive. He was dead, but He is no longer dead. He is alive, and it is therefore possible for people to encounter Him as He is and not only to remember Him as He was.

This is uniquely true of Jesus. It is true that the Bible contains stories of other persons who died and then were raised from the dead, some of them by Jesus Himself. But their case is utterly unlike that of Jesus. For after they were raised, they had to die again. They cannot be encountered by anyone today.

We might express this by saying that whereas they were resusitated, or reanimated, Jesus was resurrected. Whatever language we use, we need to recognize what the New Testament makes quite clear, namely, that what happened to Jesus on Easter is without precedent in human history. No one before Him had experienced it, nor has anyone since.

Jesus is alive. That is the first and most obvious meaning of the resurrection. Its implications are enormous.

Second, the resurrection of Christ means that God has acted in history. By a new, powerful act, God has raised His Son from the dead. This mighty act is, as it were, a new exodus or deliverance.

This act is unique. Never before had anyone been raised from the dead, never again to die.

And it is an end-time act of God. That is, the Jewish expectation, like that of many people today, was that the dead would be raised at the end of the world. They expected a general resurrection; what happened was the resurrection of one person, Jesus. And they expected it to happen at the end of history; it happened in the middle of history.

The resurrection of Jesus was the first, but not the last. The general resurrection is still a future event. But it is an event which has a precedent in the resurrection of Jesus. As Paul put it, Christ was the "firstfruits" of the resurrection (1 Cor. 15:20).

The point we must not miss is that the resurrection was an end-time act of God. That is, it marked the end of an age. The old age closed on Good Friday, and a new age was begun on Easter. By this mighty act, God inaugurated a new era in the relations between Himself and humanity.

Third, the resurrection of Christ means that God put His stamp of approval on everything that Jesus said and did.

Much of Jesus' life and teaching was validated by His miracles. But in the end, He died. And He died a death, by crucifixion, which was understood by His contemporaries to signal that God had rejected Him, even cursed Him (see Gal. 3:13). So His death put a question mark over all that had gone before. Had He told the truth? Had He been a false prophet? Had His followers been deceived?

The resurrection answered all those questions definitively. Jesus was a true prophet of the Lord. His followers were not deceived. Everything Jesus taught can be believed; God Himself, by raising His Son, validated Jesus' teaching.

In chapter 2 we noticed the puzzling fact that Jesus, though a humble man, had made Himself a part of His own message. The resurrection makes it clear that He was justified in doing that. In referring to Himself as God's Son, in calling persons to be His followers, and in requiring His disciples to remember by the Lord's Supper His passion and death, just as faithful Jews always remembered the Passover by celebrating it each year, He was only doing what He should have done. The resurrection verifies that.

The resurrection means that Jesus is alive, that God had acted uniquely and powerfully, and that everything that Jesus had said and done had received God's stamp of approval. The fourth thing that the resurrection means is that the first disciples were able to recognize and appreciate more fully who Jesus was. This is true for us as well as for Jesus' first disciples. His identity becomes clear only if we take into account that He, and He alone, has been raised from the dead.

The results of the fact that the resurrection enabled the early followers of Christ to recognize more fully who He was are the Christian gospel, the Christian faith, and the Christian church. In other words, by the event of the resurrection, a new faith was born.

If Jesus had not risen, we would in all likelihood never have known who He was. We probably would never have known that He lived! There would be no church, no gospel. At most, there might be a few Jewish people who tried to keep alive the teachings of Jesus as a rabbi, but even that is unlikely. Most probably, Jesus would today be unknown. Instead, He is known, trusted, loved, and loyally obeyed by hundreds of millions of people. The resurrection made all that possible.

Now we must explore more fully the identity of Jesus as it was revealed and confirmed by the resurrection.

Was Jesus Divine?

The first followers of Jesus were Jews. They spoke of Him in Jewish terms. In those, they made ultimate affirmations about Him.

They called Him the Christ, or Messiah, that is, God's chosen, anointed Servant and the Deliverer of His people.

They called Him the Lord. While this might mean no more than that He was a person of authority, in Jewish circles it had a special significance. The name of God in the Old Testament was Yahweh; when the Old Testament was translated into Greek, the Hebrew word *Yahweh* was translated by the Greek word *kurios,* lord. To call Jesus "Lord" was to identify Him very closely with Yahweh.

At Pentecost, in the very first post-Easter sermon, Peter said, "Let all the house of Israel therefore know assuredly that God has made him both Lord and Christ, this Jesus whom you crucified" (Acts 2:36, RSV).

These two terms, *Lord* and *Christ,* are suggestions of the way in which early Christians identified Jesus after His resurrection. They used dozens of other forms as well.[2]

What they were doing in all these affirmations was confirming their faith in Christ. This was religious faith. The attitude of the early Christians toward Christ was a religious attitude. Thomas put the words together in his great confession, "My Lord and my God" (John 20:28).[3]

If we ask how the early Christians came to have religious faith in Jesus, the answer is entirely clear: the resurrection. The resurrection was both the content of the gospel and the justification of their faith-response to Jesus.

If we ask the manner in which the early Christians affirmed their religious faith in Jesus, three things need to be said. First, they affirmed it in a Jewish manner. They used Jewish terms and concepts. Second, they affirmed it consciously. They were aware of the religious significance of what they were doing. Third, they affirmed it indirectly. They did not say directly, "Jesus is God." They said less directly, "Jesus Christ is Lord."

Why the indirection? One scholar has suggested that the Jews were such devout monotheists that a direct affirmation of Jesus as divine would have seemed to Jews a denial of the Shema, the revelation that God is one.[4] Something like this probably is the case. An indirect affirmation was adequate to the needs of the early church, and it did not create problems for monotheistic Jews so that was the ordinary form.[5]

The important thing is not, however, that the form was usually indirect. The important thing is that Jesus was the object of religious faith and that this was felt to be the appropriate response to One whom God had raised from the dead.

As we all know, the gospel about Jesus did not remain confined to Jewish people. Within a few years, the church had reached out to include non-Jews, both civilized and barbarians; Christianity thus became the first truly missionary religion and was on its way to becoming the first world religion. The world in which the Christian gospel was preached was not a vacuum. It was filled with religions and philosophies. Intellectually the most impressive force in the Roman world was the philosophy which had had its origin in Greece, being derived from such men as Socrates, Plato, and Aristotle.

The Christian faith encountered Greek philosophy openly, sometimes agreeing and sometimes disagreeing with it. Some thoughtful Christians began expressing their faith in the language and thought-categories of philosophy, particularly of Platonism. This process continued through the second, third, and fourth centuries after Christ.

Early in the fourth century, the church in Alexandria in Egypt was forced to face directly the question, Was Jesus divine? The person who forced this issue was a minister named Arius. All of his writings have been destroyed, so it is not possible to know exactly what he believed. But he seems to have felt that Christ was more than an ordinary man but less that God. He believed that God had created the worlds through Christ but that Christ was not eternal; rather He was God's first, and greatest, creation.

The bishop of Alexandria felt that this was untrue, and he attempted to silence Arius. But Arius continued to make his case. So great did the controversy become that the emperor, Constantine, called a council of bishops from all the empire to meet at Nicea, a town in Asia Minor (modern Turkey), to resolve the question. They met in AD 325.

The bishops and the emperor mostly agreed that Arius was mistaken. Their problem was that Arius was willing to say all the things which are written about Jesus in the New Testament. He believed that Jesus was Lord and Christ and the unique Son of God. The bishops could not find in the New Testament any specific affirmation about Jesus which Arius would not accept. And yet Arius clearly was not in sympathy with the fact that Jesus was divine.

In other words, the indirect affimations of the early church were no longer enough. The church now had either to say directly and explicitly that Jesus was divine or Arius and his views would have to be accepted. The decision to use more direct language than is found in the Bible was a difficult one, but they made it. They issued a creed called the Creed of Nicea, in which they said that Jesus was *homoousios,* of one and the same substance as God.

Arius could not, of course, agree to this. His teachings were declared heretical, and he was exiled.

Homoousios is a technical Greek term. It is not the language of the New Testament, the language of the end-time being fulfilled. It is the language of philosophy.

Some people have condemned the church's use of this language, calling it the Hellenizing of the simple gospel of Christ. Many modern Christians do not feel obligated to accept the teachings of the Council of Nicea. The Bible is their only authority on earth for faith and practice.

And yet, it seems to me that Nicea was essentially right, and I expect that most Christians would agree. It is true that the council used philosophical language rather than the Jewish kind of language used in the New Testament. It also is true that it is more direct than the language of the New Testament.

But it seems to me to say exactly what the New Testament said and to say what must be said about Jesus if we take His resurrection seriously. The crucified One—the One who was raised—is God. To say less than this is not to accept fully the implications of the resurrection.

Here is how one distinguished contemporary theologian has expressed it: "If these apocalyptic ideas are translated into Hellenistic terminology and conceptuality, their meaning is: in Jesus, God himself appeared on earth."[6]

That's it, exactly. If the Jewish language about Jesus—the language of resurrection, Christ, Lord—is put into Greek philosophical language, it means that Jesus was God on earth.

The message about Jesus' identity managed to move successfully from the Jewish language of end-time in the first century to the philosophical language of nature and substances in the fifth century. That language has become part of our heritage as Christians.

In our own time the confession about Jesus is in the process of being translated into another kind of language. We today do not naturally speak in Jewish terms of the end-time, but neither do we speak naturally in terms of Greek philosophy. The word *nature* does not carry for most of us today the technical meaning that *ousios* carried for the fourth-century church.

The language which is more natural to most of us today is the language of persons and interpersonal relations. And it is in that language that many of us speak most naturally about Christ.

One theologian who consciously set out to translate the Christian faith out of both Jewish and philosophical categories and into the language of persons was Leonard Hodgson, an Englishman who died in 1969. In the 1920s, he suggested that we today naturally define a human being as the subject of experiences mediated through a body in space and time. Any such subject is, by definition, a human being.

Hodgson felt that Jesus was such a subject. Only He was different from all other human beings in that He was not created to be such a subject. Rather, Jesus is the eternal Son of God, who entered into the human experience by becoming such a subject. Thus God experienced from the inside what it is to be a human being, with all the temptations, suffering, and death that involves.[7]

I believe that Hodgson found a form of words which expresses how most Christians today naturally think about Jesus. Whether we use Hodgson's exact words is not, of course, important. What matters is that we affirm that our religious faith in Jesus is justified because in Jesus God was living on earth as a man.

This is truly an amazing thing to say. It was amazing when it was said in Jewish end-time language; it was amazing when it was expressed in Greek philosophical language; and it is amazing when put in our language of persons and personal relations.

The ultimate justification for it is, and must be, the resurrection. Everything turns on that. But we might add one additional comment.

Jesus spoke of a God whose love reached to all kinds of people. He spoke of a God who seeks people like a shepherd seeking a lost sheep or like a woman searching for a lost coin (Luke 15). From the beginning, God sent leaders—Abraham, Moses, the prophets, Jesus—and took the initiative in relating to mankind.

The question is, Could such a God as Jesus described be content to send someone else? Is it not natural that eventually He would want to come Himself?

Of course, we can see this only with hindsight. It is not the sort of story which anyone would ever have imagined. We believe it because of the resurrection. But, with hindsight, we see it was suggested in Jesus' proclamation about God who loves all the world.

Now, what are the implications of this tremendous truth for our understanding of God?

The Meaning of God's Incarnation

Three things must be said about God as a result of the fact that He once became a man and dwelt among us.

First, everything that we say about Jesus, we say about God.

Thus, all the acts of Jesus were acts of God. Jesus preached, so God preached. Jesus healed, so God healed. Jesus loved, so God loved. Jesus founded a new community, so God founded a new community. Jesus was kind toward sinners and outcasts and failures, so God was also.

Again, all that Jesus experienced, God experienced. Thus, God has had the experience, in Jesus, of human birth, of growing up, of being tempted, of being hated and rejected, of suffering, and of dying. These experiences in the life of Jesus were, because He was God among us, also experiences in the life of God.

Clearly this is a tremendous fact. God knows our situation. He knows from the inside what we are going through. He did not remain secure and invulnerable in heaven and observe us from the outside. He came right down here and went through it all Himself. How He did this is a mystery, but that He did it is a wonderful truth. It might well be said to be the most important thing we know about God.

The second thing that we must say about God if we take His incarnation in Christ seriously is that the qualities which characterized Christ also characterize God. Christ was humble; God is humble! Christ was gentle; God is gentle! Christ accepted limitations in order to carry out His work. Christ expressed His strength through weakness and His wisdom through what appeared to the world to be foolishness, crucifixion; God also works through weakness and apparent foolishness. Christ came to serve, not to be served; God serves the creatures He created! Christ experienced death in order to carry out His work; God in Christ experienced death!

Clearly we are dealing with a mystery. And yet since Jesus was God incarnate, then God is humble, serving, compassionate, and so on.

I am not sure that we in the church have ever fully absorbed this meaning of incarnation. In fact, I am reasonably sure that we have not. But as we take the incarnation seriously, we may need to revise some of our understanding of God. We may learn to see God's glory, not in His power and knowledge, but in His weakness, humility, and service. In short, we see a new richness in the teaching that "God is love" (1 John 4:8).

The third thing that we must say about God if we take seriously His incarnation as Christ is that we are going to have to revise our understanding of the divine unity. Christians believe in one God, just as Jews do; but if we believe that Jesus is God and the Father is also God, then God is somehow not merely one person. More will be said about this later.

The Story of Pentecost

In this chapter we are concerned about what the New Testament reveals about God after Jesus' crucifixion and in addition to Jesus' teaching. We have been talking about how the resurrection of Jesus led the church to believe that Jesus was divine, and how taking this seriously leads us to a vast new revelation of God.

The New Testament also offers us a further understanding of God, beyond the resurrection and its implications. This further revelation was given at Pentecost.

Pentecost was a Jewish festival held fifty days after Passover. Thus, about seven weeks after Jesus' death, the disciples found themselves alone in Jerusalem. The risen Lord was no longer with them, and, following His instructions, they were waiting in Jerusalem for an additional action of God. They had a message to proclaim, the message of the risen Lord. They had a mission to carry out, to bring people to know the risen Christ and then to become part of His new community. But they lacked the power they needed to preach and carry out their mission. They were waiting for God to equip them for their work.

This He did, on Pentecost, by pouring His Spirit into their hearts. The Spirit of the Lord would guide and empower them to carry out their task (see Acts 2).

We have not said anything in this book about the Spirit before now, because, until Pentecost, it was not possible to have more than a sketchy understanding of the Spirit. But long before Pentecost, God began to prepare His people so that, when at Pentecost He finally gave them His Spirit, they would have some idea of what was happening.

Two things may be said about the preparatory revelation of the Spirit. First, God gave His Spirit to selected individuals, to give them specific gifts which would equip them to serve God in some special way. The Spirit was given only to outstanding leaders, never to ordinary persons, and always temporarily, never permanently. Among the gifts which the Spirit brought were the ability to interpret dreams (to Joseph, Gen. 41:12), craftmanship (to Bezalel, Ex. 31:2-5), military skill (to Gideon, Judg. 6:11-18), physical strength (to Samson, Judg. 13:24-25), political leadership (to Saul, 1 Sam. 9:17), and prophecy (to Micah, 3:8).

Second, a few Old Testament passages contain the promise that at some future date God will pour out His Spirit on all His people (see Joel 2:28). Those promises were never fulfilled in the Old Testament.

Similarly, two things may be said about the relation of Jesus and the Spirit. First, Jesus was the unique bearer of the Spirit. The Spirit was with Jesus permanently, guiding and empowering Him in all the aspects of His ministry. Thus Luke could write, "And Jesus returned in the power of the Spirit into Galilee" (Luke 4:14).

Second, Jesus promised His followers that someday they, too, would receive the Spirit as He Himself had (see, for example, Mark 13:11; Luke 11:13). This promise was not fulfilled during the period prior to Jesus' crucifixion.

Then on Pentecost, the great revelation of the Spirit was given. The Spirit was given to all Jesus' followers, fulfilling both His promise and the hope of the Old Testament.

Once the church had received the Spirit, they were ready to carry out their task. They now had the power and guidance they needed. Most of all, the Spirit would continually take their minds back to the facts of Jesus and His gospel. That was and is a major work of the Spirit, to remind the followers of Christ never to forget Christ (see John 15:26-27).

In the letters of Paul, we learn about the continued presence of the Spirit in the church. We may express this in a general way by saying that what Paul saw in the church was the continuation of what had begun at Pentecost. That is, as people come to faith in Christ, they received the Spirit, so that Paul could write quite clearly, "If any man have not the Spirit of Christ, he is none of his" (Rom. 8:9). The Spirit was, and is, permanently present in the life of all Christians.

Paul also elaborated some of the ways in which the Spirit empowered and guided the church in its work. Thus, for example, he bound Christians together into a community, the fellowship (*koinonia,* shared life) of the Spirit (2 Cor. 13:14). He sealed Christians so that they could never fall away from God (Eph. 1:13). He distributed gifts to all Christians so that they could be equipped to serve each other and thus to serve Christ (1 Cor. 12). And always He reminded them about Jesus.

Clearly the gift of the Spirit was a new wonderful act of God and an important revelation of God's gracious nature. But there is more to it than that.

Just as we had earlier to ask about the identity of Jesus, now we must ask about the identity of the Spirit. In the case of Jesus, since He was a human being it took the resurrection to make His followers realize that He also was God incarnate. The situation with the Spirit is different. He was not a human being, so there was no barrier to the church's coming to recognize that He is divine.

Who, then, is the Spirit? Is He an angel? An impersonal power sent from God? Is He merely an experience in the hearts of the Christians and not a reality in Himself?

To ask these questions is virtually to answer them. None of these answers will do. We know who the Spirit is. He is God.

That is why He is called the Spirit of God and the Spirit of the Lord and the Holy Spirit and the Spirit of Christ. He is the personal presence of God with His people.

Consider the situation of the earliest Christians. For about three years they had lived with Jesus. He was always present with them. They thought they had lost Him forever when He died, but He rose and came to them. Then He ascended to the Father. For ten days the disciples were in a real sense alone, waiting. Then they received the Spirit on Pentecost. And they were never alone again. The Spirit of Christ was with them. The personal presence of God was with them.

And the same is true of us today. We are not alone. God is with us. Christ is not here in His physical body, but He is present as Holy Spirit. He is in the church, and in our lives, directing and empowering us for our work.

This is a wonderful gift of God—His personal presence. It also is an important new revelation of God. It leads us to inquire even further concerning the nature of the divine unity, for now we know God as

Father, as Christ, and as Spirit. We shall look into this matter further in the final chapter of this book.

The New Revelation of God

How might we go about summarizing the revelation which God gave of Himself following the crucifixion of Jesus? We will do so by returning to the four kinds of development which we observed in the Old Testament revelation of God.

First, in the Old Testament, there was a movement away from seeing God primarily in nature to seeing Him primarily in history, in events, such as the Exodus. In the New Testament, that movement continued and became more specific. The event in history which became the definitive revelation of God, is the event of Jesus. By looking at Jesus, we learn more about God than in any other revelation.

Second, in the Old Testament there was a movement from ritualism to morality. This continued in the New Testament, and it was much needed. For the emphasis on morality had degenerated into moralism, the idea that persons can earn God's approval by being good or keeping the law. In the New Testament, we learn of the grace of a God who loves and accepts not only the morally upright but also the morally and religiously bankrupt.

Third, in the Old Testament, we noticed a movement beyond a national understanding of God toward seeing God as the universal God of all people. The New Testament takes this development even further and portrays the new community, the church, as a missionary force, reaching out to all people to tell them that their true Creator, the only true and living God, is the Father of Jesus Christ.

Finally, in the Old Testament, we observed a movement away from polytheism to monotheism. The New Testament takes this movement further also, revealing to us that the one God has a rich inner life as Father, Son, and Spirit.

This concludes our examination of God's self-relevation in the Bible and in Christ. Many other things could be said, but these are some representative and important revelations of God to us. Our next

task will be to attempt to construct a coherent and illuminating understanding of God out of these biblical resources. In other words, we
shall attempt now to paint a verbal portrait of the God who so
graciously revealed Himself to us in the Old Testament, in Jesus, and
in the New Testament.

Notes

1. An excellent essay on this is "The Events of Easter and the Empty
Tomb" by Hans von Campenhausen, printed in *Tradition and Life in the
Early Church.*

2. Christology is the central issue in the study of New Testament theology.
Hundreds of books exist on this complex topic. My own understanding owes
much to many books; I would single out *The Origin of Christology* by C. F.
D. Moule (Cambridge) as a helpful, balanced study.

3. See William Hendricks, *Who Is Jesus Christ?* "Layman's Library of
Christian Doctrine." 2 (Nashville: Broadman Press, 1985).

4. Anthony Hanson, "Symbolism and the Doctrine of God," *London Quat-
erly and Holborn Review* (July, 1964), p. 182.

5. Some New Testament terminology is more direct than others. One of the
most direct is found in Thomas's confessing to the risen Christ, "My Lord
and my God" (John 20:28).

6. Wolfhart Pannenberg, *Jesus—God and Man,* p. 69.

7. Hodgson developed these ideas in several places, including his book *And
Was Made Man* (1928) and "The Incarnation" in *Essays on the Trinity and
Incarnation* edited by A. E. J. Rawlinson (1928).

Part II
Doctrinal

In Part I we reviewed the revelation which God gave of Himself in Jesus and in the Bible. Our work was largely exploratory.

In Part II, we shall attempt to give a verbal portrait of God in the language of the twentieth-century church. Our work will be largely constructive.

In one sense, our task is a simple one; all that we have to do is to arrange the biblical revelation in an order that contemporary Christians will find meaningful.

But in another sense, our task is a difficult one. How could anyone begin to sketch a verbal portrait of God?

It seems to me that the best hint about how to proceed is this: Sketch your portrait of God along the lines you would follow if you were asked to sketch the portrait of a friend.

How would you go about describing a friend to someone who did not know him or her?

First, you might give some of the most basic information. You might say something such as, "She is a married woman, my age, who lives down the street from me."

Next, you might tell about her goals in life. For example, "She hopes to combine a career in law with being an effective homemaker and a loving wife and mother."

Then you might tell about some of the activities by which your friend is attempting to achieve her goals. For example, "She attends law school at night; she studies during the day while her boys are in school; she types her papers on a word processor; she has taught her boys to clean up their rooms; she has bought a dishwasher; and she spends all her summers with her family."

Finally, you might use some adjectives to describe your friend. You probably would not draw up long lists of adjectives, but rather you would select the most pertinent ones. For example, "She is ambitious, energetic, well-organized, and devoted to her family even more than to her career."

In Part II, we shall follow this arrangement in order to attempt a portrait of God. We shall speak first of His fundamental nature, then of His purpose, then of His activities, and finally of His character.

4

God as Both Like and Unlike Human Beings

The title of this chapter requires a brief explanation. My purpose in this chapter is to sketch what is fundamental about God. In traditional terms, our concern now is for the nature of God.

In order to do justice to this matter, it is necessary to speak of two factors. They may be called the personhood and the transcendence of God.

God's personhood is that dimension of His nature which is most like human beings. We are personal; God is like us, personal.

God's transcendence is that dimension of God's nature which is least like human beings. God utterly transcends us; God is unlike us.

We begin with the personhood of God.

God Is Personal

In the first three chapters of this book, I spoke of God's self-revelation in Jesus and in the Bible. Everything I said about God in those chapters either presupposed or directly asserted that God is personal. He is Someone, not Something. God is not an It; God is a He.[1]

To affirm that God is personal is to employ a distinction between persons and things. It is a commonsense distinction. Virtually all adults in our society recognize it.

It is a distinction that is learned, not innate. Children are not born with it. In their early years, they sometimes confuse persons and things. For example, a child may express more affection for a doll than for another child. But eventually most people get the distinction straight.

The distinction is sometimes forgotten. For example, an elderly couple may lavish more attention on a poodle than on one another. We are all tempted to use persons and to love things, when the appropriate behavior is to love persons and to use things.

But it is basically a clear distinction. To say that God is personal is to say that He is far more like a person than like a thing. The Bible everywhere does this. In addition to all these things which we have already said about God's self-revelation as personal, two other things may be noted.

First, the Bible frequently uses anthropomorphisms in speaking of God. *Anthropos* is Greek for "man," and *morphē* is Greek for "form." An anthropomorphism is a reference to God as being in the form of a man, or like a person.

The Bible has many of these. God is a Father, a Shepherd, a King. God walks, talks, speaks, listens, plans, and acts.

The writers of the Bible occasionally employed nonpersonal language about God. Thus a psalmist wrote, "The Lord is my rock and fortress" (Ps. 18:2).

Which of the two kinds of language, the personal or the nonpersonal, was more basic in the Bible? To ask the question is to answer it. God is personal. It is not that God is basically like a rock or a fortress, which the psalmist then personified. Rather, God is basically personal, and the psalmist used a bit of nonpersonal language in order to speak of God as his protector, his guardian.

Second, the account of creation in Genesis 1 records that God created human beings in His own image. If mankind is created in God's image, it is hardly surprising that when they think about God they will think of Him as being like themselves in some sense.

What is the image of God? Students of the Bible have debated this for centuries. It has been suggested that the image of God is our reason, or our moral sense, or our creativity, or our capacity for love relationships. The reason that we have been free to speculate about the image of God is that the Bible never says precisely what the image of God is.

I want to offer a suggestion about the image of God. I would suggest that in Genesis, the image of God is what sets human beings apart from all the rest of God's creation. It is that which is unique about people; it is that which distinguishes persons from things.

In modern English, we have a word for what is unique about people. It is the word *personal.*

Therefore, I would suggest that there is a rough correspondence between "the image of God" and "personal." If this be accepted, we are free to explore what is unique about persons and to associate those things with the image of God. They would doubtless include our reason, moral judgment, creativity, and capacity for love. To these could be added other factors, such as freedom, self-consciousness, and so on.

In all the divine self-revelation in the Bible, including its affirmation that mankind is in God's image and its employment of anthropomorphisms, God is treated as personal. The importance of this cannot be exaggerated. Since God is personal, religion is possible. Revelation is understandable. Prayer is sensible. Worship is appropriate. Moral obedience is reasonable.

On the other hand, if God were not personal, then prayer would be no more than self-therapy. Worship would be contrived or cowardly. Moral obedience would be irrelevant.

Clearly a great deal rides on whether we think of God as personal.

God Is Transcendent

In order to speak responsibly of what is most fundamental about God, we cannot say that God is personal and stop at that; we must add that God is transcendent. He is beyond personhood as we experience it in other people.

If we acknowledge God's personhood but fail to acknowledge His transcendence, we could be bringing God down to the level of human beings. In that case, God would not really be God, but just a human being. He might perhaps be the oldest, wisest, most powerful human being, but He would still be no more than a human being.

But God is much more than a human being. He is God. He is the Other. He is beyond human beings.

In short, God is both like us, personal, and unlike us, utterly transcendent.

One biblical term which refers to God's transcendence is *holy*. Orginally *holy* did not mean "righteous" or "good." It meant "the transcendent," "the mysterious," "the awesome." To say that God is holy is to say that He is utterly unlike any of His creation, even human beings.

The most famous book to have appeared on this subject in the twentieth century is probably *The Idea of the Holy* by Rudolf Otto. Otto believed that the fundamental religious experience is the experience of that which is awesome and overwhelming. He referred to the Holy with a Latin phrase, *mysterium tremendum et fascinans,* the mystery which is both awesome and fascinating. Persons who encounter God in His otherness are both overwhelmed by and attracted to God.

I have chosen to use the word *transcendent* for this aspect of God's nature because I believe that it more nearly communicates the sense we intend than any other term I know.

In using it in this way, I am departing from its traditional use in theology. Traditionally *transcendent* was paired with *immanent* to describe God's spatial presence. The two terms meant that God is both beyond the universe, spatially, and present at every point in the universe, spatially. I do not believe that God's relationship to space is a major concern of most people today; everyone pretty much understands that God does not have a body and so is not spatially bound (see John 4:24). So I have enlisted the word *transcendent* to fill the more fundamental role of affirming that God is beyond personhood as we experience it in human beings.

Other terms can help also. For example, God is infinite. That is, He has no limitations. In this He is utterly unlike human beings, who are finite, limited.

Again, God is utterly free. Nothing outside Himself places any constraints on God. In this He is quite unlike human beings, whose lives are characterized in large measure by their constraints. Thus we might say of a person that she is a woman (and thus not a man), of advanced years (not young), who speaks English (not Russian), who lives in the United States (not Australia), and so on. Human beings are always bound; God is utterly free from all external limitations. He transcends the kinds of limitations which are inescapably a part of the makeup of human beings.

Can God Be Both Like and Unlike Us?

We have affirmed that God is fundamentally like us, personal, and also that He is fundamentally unlike us, transcendent. Have we contradicted ourselves? Can both these affirmations be true?

Theologians and philosophers are quite aware that it is difficult to reconcile the two affirmations. A Christian philosopher, C. C. J. Webb, expressed it this way:

> A modern controversy about "the personality of God" will be found to turn upon the difficulty involved in reconciling the finitude which seems to be essential to human personality with the absoluteness and infinity, or at least omnipresence and omnipotence, which we are accustomed to ascribe to God.[2]

The problem is that it is difficult to see how God could be personal and yet transcend all limitations, since limitations are so characteristic of ourselves and of all the other persons (human beings) we encounter in daily life.

Some theologians feel this problem so acutely that they attempt to resolve it by denying or at least minimizing either God's personhood or His transcedence.

A theologian who allowed God's personhood to go into eclipse was Paul Tillich. He wrote a book entitled *Biblical Religion and the Search for Ultimate Reality* in which he intended to reconcile biblical religion, with its stress on God's personhood, with the philosophical, human quest for an Ultimate Reality understood as nonpersonal.

Tillich was a profound thinker and his ideas in this little book are complex, but in my judgment he reconciled these two at the expense of God's personhood. Thus he wrote: "The God who is *a* being is transcended by the God who is Being Itself, the ground and abyss of every being. And the God who is a person is transcended by the God who is the Personal-Itself, the ground and abyss of every person."[3]

As I said, Tillich's ideas are complex, but here it seems to me that he has, in fact, forfeited God's personhood in order to make room for the utter transcendence of God. He seems to have felt that it was not possible for God to be genuinely personal (*a* person, to use his language) and also genuinely transcendent.

Earlier in our century, a group of theologians known as the Boston personalists argued vigorously for the personhood of God. But, like Tillich, some of them seem to have felt that authentic personhood and authentic transcendence were not compatible, so they allowed God's transcendence to go into eclipse. They spoke of God as finite.

Traditional Christian language about God has been a blend of the personal and the transcendent. For example, Jesus spoke of the "holy Father." As holy, God is utterly unlike human beings; as Father, He is like us, personal (see John 17:25). Again, Jesus taught His followers to pray: "Our Father which art in heaven" (Matt. 6:9). As Father, God is like us, personal; as "in heaven," God utterly transcends us, is unlike us.

How might we go about understanding the compatibility of these two dimensions of God's nature? I would offer three suggestions.

First, we might point out that one human being may be both like and unlike a second human being.

Imagine two men, Jones and Smith. We could say that Jones is very much like Smith and also utterly unlike Smith. Is this nonsense?

Not at all. For example, both Jones and Smith could be utterly devoted husbands and fathers. Each could love his wife and children intensely. Each could express his love for his family in words and deeds.

But Jones and Smith might be entirely different in some other regard. For example, Jones might be an indoors person. He might love air-conditioned buildings and hate the out-of-doors. He might be a city person, and a night person, and hate to go to work before ten in the morning. He might peel in the sun and freeze in November. His idea of the worst place on earth might be a deer camp, and of the worst experience of his life, a fishing trip. He might wear a vested suit and a shirt with a button-down collar to go to the movies.

Smith, on the other hand, might be a born outdoorsman. His favorite magazine might be on outdoors subjects. He might earn his living putting roofing on houses, and his fondest dream might be to own his own farm. On vacations he might take his family backpacking, and they might begin at five o'clock each morning. He might not own a suit or tie; he might wear denims and flannel shirts to church. He might live in the countryside, going to the city only to work, and never staying in a closed-up building longer than necessary.

Jones and Smith are entirely alike as husbands and fathers, entirely unlike temperamentally and vocationally. It is by no means nonsense to say that Jones is both like and unlike Smith.

The illustration does not, of course, prove that God is both like and unlike human beings, both personal and transcendent. But it shows that it is not always unreasonable to suggest that someone may be both like and unlike another.

It could be said that Jones is like Smith with reference to some specific matters (family) and unlike Smith with reference to other specific matters (vocational preference). Then it could be asked, in what ways is God like us and in what ways unlike us? Here the analogy is limited. For God is like us—personal—in all matters and He is unlike us—transcendent—in all matters also. So the story is an illustration, not a proof.

A second help in understanding the compatibility of the personhood and transcendence of God is to say that human beings actually encounter God as both personal and transcendent. In making this observation, no effort is made to provide a rational reconciliation of the two; instead, it is simply pointed out that the surrender of either dimension of God's experience of God is untrue to our actual experience.

This too is a helpful procedure. It was followed by Rudolf Otto, and there is no reason that it cannot be followed today. It shifts the burden of proof from the traditional Christian to the person who assumes that personhood and transcendence are incompatible; for if in religion we encounter God as both, then either one must accept that He is both or else demonstrate that our experience is not what it seems to be.

One other thing can be said. A case can be made for the fact that, so far from being incompatible, one dimension of God's nature actually requires the other. Specifically, God's utter transcendence requires that He be personal.

Here is how one twentieth-century theologian expressed this point: "Which limits God more—to say that He does have the capacity for fellowship, which is what personality is, or to say that He does not have it?"[4] In other words, can you affirm God's transcendence without also affirming His personhood? For if He is not personal, is He not then limited indeed, even more limited than we who are personal, and thus very far from being transcendent?

I myself believe very deeply that God is both personal and transcendent. I do not feel that these two aspects of His nature are incompatible. I believe that our deepest religious experiences lead us to recognize both. And I concur with the late Professor Mackintosh that if God were not personal He would not be transcendent. He is both. That is His nature.

Now I will attempt to identify the religious importance of the subject which I have been discussing in a somewhat abstract manner.

Responding to God

No one knows God fully; but it is possible to know Him in a balanced, though limited, way. A balanced knowledge of God recognizes both His personhood and His transcendence. It senses God's intimacy and also His mystery. It finds God winsome and also awesome.

And it responds to God appropriately. To the personhood of God, it responds with loyalty, confidence, and personal devotion. It does not attempt to manipulate God because it is inappropriate to try to manipulate persons. It loves God and does not try to use Him.

A balanced knowledge of God responds to God's transcendence with awe, reverence, and humility. It does not attempt to manipulate God because it knows that it is impossible to manipulate the utterly transcendent One. It respects God and does not try to use Him.

It is difficult to express in words how one with a balanced understanding of God responds religiously to God. The response is intimate without being familiar or presumptuous; it is reverent without being cold or formal. It celebrates its clear understanding of the God who has graciously revealed Himself, and it also celebrates the mystery of the holy Lord who is beyond us. The response is natural but not casual, bold but not pushy, humble but not craven, respectful but not terrified.

These descriptions are only partial, and they describe an ideal rather than an actual response. We strive for them but do not always achieve them. It is always possible that we will fail to respond to God as we should, by allowing ourselves to respond to one dimension of His nature but not the other. What we must do is to cultivate the balance we need. Perhaps the best place to begin is with the Lord's Prayer which is a perfect example of recognizing both God's personhood and His transcendence.

Notes

1. The Bible usually presents God as male. In a few references, God is presented as female; in Isaiah 45:10, for example, God is like a woman giving birth, and in Luke 15:8-9, God is like a woman searching for a lost coin. God transcends sexuality.

2. C. C. J. Webb, *Problems in the Relations of God and Men*, p. 216.

3. Paul Tillich, *Biblical Religion and the Search for Ultimate Reality* pp. 82-83.

4. H. R. Mackintosh, *The Christian Apprehension of God*, p. 136.

5
The Purpose of God

Persons and Their Purposes

One of the most important things to know about a person is what his purposes are. Few things tell you more about someone than to have an idea of his intention.

The same thing is true of God. One of the most valuable insights into what God is like is to become informed about His purposes. If we can catch a glimpse of why God created the world and why He has acted when and as He has, our understanding of Him will be increased enormously.

Oddly enough, theologians have not always been very specific about the divine purpose. This is surprising because the Bible contains frequent references to God's purpose. Probably several things have contributed to the neglect of this subject by the theologians.

Before we consider some of what has been said on this subject, we need to recognize that people in our time are more likely to have a personal acquaintance with the idea of adopting purposes for one's own life than people in the past. It seems likely that before the industrial revolution, only relatively few people had the opportunity of freely choosing many of their own goals in life. Life expectancy was much shorter then than now. Personal freedoms were generally more restricted than they are today. The range of occupational choices was much narrower. Travel was restricted, so that the choice of one's wife or husband was more limited. In general, the idea of a person freely setting personal goals and carrying them out was restricted to a much smaller proportion of the population than today.

Perhaps it is the widespread awareness of the possibility of personal goal-setting which makes us today more conscious of how important it is to understand a person's purposes if we are to understand him. And we easily carry over this idea into our understanding of God.

Suggestions About God's Purpose

Several suggestions have been made in the church concerning God's purpose. One that is often voiced is that God's purpose is a mystery.

This certainly is true, and nothing in this chapter is intended to imply otherwise. There is a mystery about God and all His purposes and activities. I spoke in the last chapter of God's transcendence; it is inevitable that mystery will always surround the Transcendent One.

But we might ask how the affirmation of the mystery of God's purpose is being used when this is said. Is it being used to lead us to worship? Or is it being used to prevent us from inquiring into God's purpose? We welcome the impetus for worship, but we question the wisdom of forestalling a look at God's purpose.

Of course, we must approach God's purpose with humility. But suppose God wants us to know about His purpose. Suppose He reveals it to us and makes provision for us to understand it. Would it then be humility to refuse to try to understand it? Not at all. It would be refusing a divine revelation.

My conviction is that in fact, God has revealed His purpose to us; He wants us to understand what He intends. We ought to make what effort we can to understand. Then, when we have grasped what we can, we are likely to be keenly aware of the mystery of God's purpose. In fact, we may never be fully aware of the mystery of it until we have made our best effort to understand.

A second thing that traditionally has been said about God's purpose is that His purpose is to save sinners. This affirmation is found among all Christians, and it is emphasized among Christians who put a high priority on evangelism.

Like the statement that God's purpose is a mystery, this too is a true statement. It is indeed God's purpose to save sinners.

But for what? We tend to stress what God saves sinners from, namely, sin and judgment and death. But what does He save them to?

I would suggest that salvation is a means to a end, not an end in itself. And until we have some notion of what the end is, there is something unsatisfying about saying that the purpose of God is to save sinners. It's a little like asking a student what his purpose in life is and being told that his purpose is to study and to prepare himself for work; until you know what kind of work (engineering? sales? management?), you don't feel that you've learned much.

A third suggestion concerning God's purpose is that He intends to bring glory to Himself. Like the two earlier answers, this one is true. And also like them, it is not fully satisfying. In fact, it is a problematic answer.

First we want to clarify what is meant by glory being given to God. It does not mean that God's glory is increased. God is all-glorious. He is perfect in glory and beauty. Nothing can add anything to His glory. He did not add to His glory by creating the world, nor do we add anything to His glory by our worship or service. Therefore to say that God's purpose is to bring glory to Himself does not mean that God intends to become more glorious.

Rather, the phrase "glorify God" means that God's creatures recognize, acknowledge, and confess His glory. They celebrate God's glory in their worship.

Now, can we say that God's purpose in creation is to make persons who will celebrate His glory by worshiping Him? Indeed we can say this. It is a true and important thing.

It also is, in my judgment, an ultimate thing. In other words, it is something which needs to be said at the end of our statement concerning God's purpose. If we say it too soon, it seems to me that we create a misunderstanding. We seem to suggest that God is very self-centered.

It is difficult to put the problem into words without seeming irreverent, and I do not want to be irreverent. So, I will offer a quotation from a contemporary writer, J. B. Priestley, who had pretty much lost his faith in God by the time of his death in 1984. In his autobiography entitled *Instead of the Trees,* he wrote: "I for one shrink from a God whose only idea is to hear Himself endlessly praised."[1]

Now when we Christians read something like this, we tend to respond in one of two ways. Some us tend to want to say that Priestly had better accept that God is at the center of things. We tend to want to insist that, like it or not, that is the way it is. God is God, and Priestly will be in trouble if he refuses to submit to that fact.

This is an entirely understandable reaction. However, some Christians tend to react in a different way.

They tend to say that Priestly has misunderstood. He has failed to get the true picture. If he understood the situation better, he would not have written those words.

For, they insist, God is ultimately concerned about human beings. He is committed to them. They are at the center of His love and interest. If Priestley could see that, he would soon realize that God's purpose is indeed a noble one.

My sympathies are with the second reaction. I feel that people like Priestley resist God's purpose because they have misunderstood it. If they could only understand better God's love and concern for us, they would be able to get the true sense of His purpose.

We have seen that three answers are usually given when we ask about the purpose of God. Each is true. But each also is partial and unsatisfying. Could it be that something else needs to be said which would be more satisfying and which would help us to appreciate these three answers better? I think so.

A Contemporary Statement

There is a phrase which is often used in the church which seems to me to provide the clue we need in order to spell out more fully the purpose of God. It is a phrase which usually is used in connection with the doctrine of creation: "God created man for fellowship with himself." It is not taken directly from the Bible, but it certainly seems to me to be true to the Bible.

The needed clue for speaking about God's purpose is the idea of God and persons being in fellowship. This immediately suggests the Old Testament idea of covenant. It suggests the creation of a community. It also suggests the priority of love.

I would express my own understanding of God's purpose as follows: God's purpose is to create a community of persons who freely choose to accept God as their God, who receive His love into their lives, and who respond by loving Him with all their hearts and by loving their neighbors as themselves.

There are several essential components of this understanding of God's purpose. One is community; another is freedom; another is that God is accepted as God; another, that the fundamental response to God's love is to love God and others.

Of course, this is a limited statement of God's purpose. It certainly is not complete. Perhaps its emphases are not what they should be. But it seems to me to be balanced and to gather into one sentence the most important things we know about God's purpose.

One factor in support of this statement is that it provides a place for each of the traditional statements and, in fact enriches them; and it also manages to avoid the problems associated with them.

Thus, this statement provides an answer to the question which dogs the statement, God's purpose is to save sinners. The question which that statement raises is, Save for what? Our statement says, Save for participation in a new community of love and trust between God and mankind.

It also helps with the problem raised by the statement, God's purpose is to bring glory to himself. It shows that God is not at all self-centered. He is concerned about human beings and their freedom. He wants them to accept Him as God, which is only right since He is God. God wants His love to be poured out on His people, drawing from them a response of love for Him and for others.

For this incomparable love, people will glorify God forever. They will not have been coerced into this, nor will they do it resentfully. Having benefited from God's purpose and love so fully, it will be only natural and reasonable that they will worship Him for including them in such a gracious purpose. We might put it this way: Since we have seen in Christ that we human beings are at the center of God's love and attention, we find it natural for God to be at the center of our love and attention.

Finally, it is this purpose—to create a community of persons who freely accept God and His love and who love Him and others in return—which is such a mystery. The mystery of God's purpose is not that we know nothing about it. The mystery is that we do know about it and that it is difficult to understand why God has chosen to include us in His circle of love, in His family so to speak.

Some people have suggested that God has done this because in some sense He needs us. I think this is not likely. It seems to me that He has done this for our benefit entirely, not for His. That is the mystery of a love which creates persons in order to pour out His love upon them.

We might elaborate our understanding of the divine purpose by saying that the material universe is a stage on which the drama of human existence is being acted out. The central action of the drama is the creation of a community of love and trust. The author of the drama is God; and at one point He Himself appeared on the stage as a central character, Jesus. The conclusion of the drama was known to Him, but the struggles which were necessary in order for the conclusion to be reached were real nevertheless.

The Revelation of the Divine Purpose

The definition of the divine purpose which I am proposing contains a number of biblical ingredients, including God's concern for persons, His creation of a covenant community, His provision for salvation, and the priority of love in human life. In one sense, the formulation of God's purpose is the theme of all the Bible. This definition attempts merely to bring together in one statement many of the biblical allusions to God's purpose.

But the Bible also contains some rather direct language about God's purpose. Two examples will be given.

The first is the kingdom of God as Jesus proclaimed it. The kingdom is God's sovereign rule. It is offered by Jesus through His work and received by anyone—absolutely anyone—who will open his life to it. The result was a new people of God bound together with Him in a covenant of love. That was Jesus' way of expressing the purpose of God.

A second direct statement about God's purpose is found in the Letter to the Ephesians. A major theme of that letter is the will of God. The will of God is God's purpose in creating the world. Here is a representative passage:

> Blessed be the God and Father of our Lord Jesus Christ, who hath blessed us with all spiritual blessings in heavenly places in Christ: According as he hath chosen us in him before the foundation of the world, that we should be holy and without blame before him in love: Having predestinated us unto the adoption of children by Jesus Christ to himself, according to the good pleasure of his will, To the praise of the glory of his grace, wherein he hath made us accepted in the beloved. In whom we have redemption through his blood, the forgiveness of sins, according to the riches of his grace; Wherein he hath abounded toward us in all wisdom and prudence; Having made known unto us the mystery of his will, according to his good pleasure which he hath purposed in himself: That in the dispensation of the fulness of times he might gather together in one all things in Christ, both which are on earth; even in him: In whom also we have obtained an inheritance, being predestinated according to the purpose of him who worketh all things after the counsel of his own will: That we should be to the praise of his glory, who first trusted in Christ. In whom ye also trusted, after that ye heard the word of truth, the gospel of your salvation: in whom also after that ye believed, ye were sealed with that holy Spirit of promise, Which is the earnest of our inheritance until the redemption of the purchased possession, unto the praise of his glory (1:3-14).

Now we will consider briefly some practical implications of our understanding of God's purpose.

Understanding Ourselves and God

In recent years a number of philosophers became engaged in a debate about what they sometimes call QML, the question of the meaning of life. The philosophy known as existentialism placed this question on the agenda of philosophical discussion. Christians have taken advantage of this interest and have insisted that the meaning of life is found only in God. Some non-Christian philosophers responded to this by insisting that human life can be rich and meaningful even for those who have no religious faith.[2]

It would be unwise to say that this question is easily resolved. But I believe that we can responsibly say this, that human life has a meaning if there is a God who loves and purposes love, that it does not have if there be no such God. We can put the same thing in terms of our experience; we who believe in God as He revealed Himself in Jesus and the Bible understand our lives to possess a meaning and purpose which those without our faith do not experience. In fact, we believe that the true destiny of every human being is to participate in the community that God is creating, though unfortunately many are unaware of this and are even rejecting their true destiny.

So one very important implication of the purpose of God is that it gives to our lives an ultimate meaning which they would not have if this were not God's purpose. There is a value to our lives, a reason for our existence, and a dignity to all we are and do that derives only from the belief that we are included in the eternal purpose of God.

The same thing is true of the entire universe, and this is the second implication of the divine purpose. The universe is not meaningless. It is not merely the movement of atoms. Life on our planet is not an accident of blind evolutionary forces. Human beings are not merely complex organisms. Nature is not merely a matter of the survival of the fittest. History is not merely a humiliating dance in which the strong and fortunate assert their dominance and the others submit to the inevitable. It is not all a chaos.

The universe is a cosmos. It is a world with a purpose. History is going somewhere. There is a purpose for every human being on earth.

That purpose is to become part of the community which God is creating, to experience God's love, and to learn to love God and others.

The third implication of the purpose of God concerns God Himself. To know the chief purpose of a human being is to understand Him better. Similarly, to know the purpose of God is to understand Him better.

This, then, is the God we know and love, a God who created a world in order to create a community on whom to shower His love. He respects the freedom of human beings, allowing them to decide for themselves whether they will be His people. He offers His grace and helps to rescue people from their predicament and to transform them into lovers. He elicits from them the response of love—love of Him, of course, and love of one another.

How wonderful our God is! He is gracious beyond our power to describe. He has included us, creatures of His hand, in His eternal purpose. He begins to carry out His purpose in our history and experience, and He continues it in eternity.

The purpose of God should always serve as a fixed point in our theology. We must not get lost in the details of our ideas so that we lose sight of the overall purpose. We should go back again and again in our minds to this great truth and maintain it steadily: God is creating a family of persons to be His own, persons who freely accept Him as God and receive His grace into their lives, persons who are learning to respond to God by loving Him with all their hearts and by loving others as themselves.

Notes

1. J. B. Priestly, *Instead of the Trees,* p. 114.
2. See, for example, E. D. Klempke, ed., *The Meaning of Life,* p. 173.

6

The Activities of God

Why God Acts

Our constructive statement about God now contains two principal affirmations. First, God is both like and unlike us; in other words, He is the Transcendent One. Second, God's purpose is to create a family of persons who freely accept Him as God and receive His love and who respond by loving Him and one another.

Now let us look at how God's purpose is to be fulfilled. There seem to be three possibilities.

First, it is possible that once God had created free persons they might naturally open their lives to His love and to loving one another. Theoretically, this would seem to be possible. We might even speculate that it has occurred in some universe unknown to us.

Whether or not that is true, it certainly has not occurred in the world of our experience. God's purpose is not being achieved naturally by the inhabitants of planet Earth. Human beings do not love each other as themselves. They do not love God with all their hearts. They do not fully accept God as God. Nor do they naturally come together as one great family.

These remarks are not intended to be cynical. Human beings often do good and wonderful things, and for this we are grateful. I do not want to deny that there is any good in us. There is much good.

And yet, human beings are facing a serious predicament. There is no need to overstate this predicament. It is widely recognized that, though there is much good on earth, we human beings have made a real mess of things. Our world is characterized by greed, violence, deceit, rage, war, suspicion, self-centeredness, guilt, suffering, and finally death.

In short, God's great purpose is not naturally being carried out among us. We may assume, therefore, that if it is to be fulfilled, it will be because God has acted to make it happen.

The second possibility is that God will call upon His great knowledge and power and carry out His purpose by force. We assume that He who has power sufficient to create and control the universe has enough power to coerce human beings into conforming to His intentions for them.

This is an attractive suggestion, especially in light of the serious predicament of human beings. Perhaps there is some truth in it.

But as a statement of the general way in which God's purpose will be fulfilled, it is not acceptable. The reason for this is that it is not possible for God to coerce persons into a free acceptance of Him and His love. Freedom and coercion are mutually exclusive. If God intends to create a community of free persons, then by definition He will not use coercion to bring this about.

To say that God cannot coerce a free response from human beings does not imply that God's power is inadequate. It is a logical contradiction to speak of free responses being coerced, just as it is a logical contradiction to speak of a square with three sides. A logical contradiction is nonsense; to say that God cannot do something which is nonsense does not imply a deficiency in His power.

This brings us to the third possibility. If human beings do not naturally fulfill God's purpose, and if it is self-contradictory to suggest that God could coerce a free response from people, one other option is available. It is that God acts by persuasion rather than coercion. It is that He acts, effectively but patiently, in ways that do not override human freedom, to entice a free response of love from human beings.

It seems to me that this is exactly how God has acted. He has not forced people to participate in His purpose. He has not bludgeoned us into servile submission. He has not brainwashed us or tricked us or manipulated us into becoming a community of His own. He does not intimidate people to love Him or condition them into a reflexive reaction of community life.

Rather, He restrains His power so that people have a margin of freedom. It is with that freedom that they choose to become His people or not. God protects human beings and their freedom; He respects their freedom.

But God does act. He acts in love. By love He wins the hearts of men and women and children. People are attracted to the love of God.

The power which is most characteristic of God's acts is not the power of raw force. It is the power of love. The wisdom which is most characteristic of God's acts in not the wisdom of raw factual knowledge. It is the wisdom of love.

Because God always acts with a love which respects human freedom, He never uses coercion; rather He elicits a free response of love. The result is that His purpose is being carried out. By acting in this way, God progressively fulfills His intention to create a community of free persons who accept Him as God and receive His love in their lives and who love Him with all their hearts and love others as themselves.

Now we will look briefly at the acts of preparation, implementation, and consummation by which God fulfills His purpose.

Preparation

Two acts of God are preparatory to the carrying out of His purpose. The first is the creation of the natural world; the second is the creation of the particular creature man, who is free to accept or reject God and His love.

In our examination of the Old Testament, we observed the revelation of God as Creator. I do not intend to repeat here what was said there. One additional comment is in order. It concerns the relationship between the natural world and mankind.

Earlier we spoke of the world as a stage on which the drama of human existence is being acted out. This metaphor implies an entirely clear distinction between human beings and nature. Nature is the stage; people are the actors.

Actually, things are a bit more involved than that. For man is very much a part of the natural world. He was created from the dust (Gen. 2:7), and he never gets far away from the natural world. It is clear that human beings are involved in nature.

Therefore we may ask if it is correct to make such a clear distinction between mankind and nature. My feeling is that this is justified. While I find the continuity between mankind and nature an interesting subject, I find the discontinuity even more interesting. The biblical record of God's acts shows God as interested in the natural world, but without question His interest centers upon humanity rather than nature. Paul referred on one occasion to the redemption of all creation (Rom. 8:21-22), but he wrote many dozens of times of the redemption of mankind. We may suppose that the redemption of nature is a corollary to and by-product of the redemption of mankind.

All this is not intended to be a statement against ecology, or, as we used to say, conservation. To seek to maintain the beauty of natural forests and the survival of animal and plant life is a wonderful thing. To resist the pollution of our air and water and soil is good.

But the ultimate reason that ecology is good is that it serves the best interests of human beings. Nature is not an end in itself. It is of value because it supports human existence. Natural resources are precisely that, resources provided by God for mankind in nature.

The second great preparatory act was the creation of the unique creatures called human beings. Three things may be said about the creation of human beings in connection with God's purpose.

First, God created human beings to be free. That was essential to His purpose. This does not mean that human freedom has no restraints. In fact, human freedom is always circumscribed, never absolute. All people are not equally free. An individual does not always experience freedom fully; at times one may be more free, at other times less. Human beings are variously conditioned and determined.

But always there remains a margin of freedom. God created it, and He respects it. And it is that freedom which enables people either to accept or to reject God and His love.

Second, God created human beings who are capable of community, of religious faith, and of love. These capacities are essential to the carrying out of God's purpose. They vary greatly from one person to the next. They can be distorted, as when a community is formed to be elitist or when worship is directed toward idols or when love becomes controlling and possessive. But the capacity is there in all human beings.

Third, God gives all people an inclination toward their free destiny. He plants a hunger in their hearts to participate in a community of love and trust toward God. We all lean toward God's purpose for us. As Augustine put it in a prayer, "You have made us for yourself, and our hearts are restless till they find their rest in you" (*Confessions,* I, 1).

Of course, we are by no means always aware of this inclination in us. We can squelch it, direct it toward something other than God, ignore it, or otherwise fail to follow through in it. When we do this, we continue to feel a sense of incompleteness, restlessness, and dissatisfaction. Whether a person ever loses this inclination for God, I do not know. To lose it would be the ultimate tragedy for a human being.

Also, the reverse is true. When you freely open your heart to God and come into community, you receive a deep sense of having begun to fulfill your true destiny. This sense is difficult to to describe; it does not overwhelm you and, strictly speaking, does not prove the truth of the Christian religion. But in your heart you know that you have come home.

We have been speaking of the preparatory work God does in order to carry out His purposes. It includes creating a natural world within which persons can live and creating persons who are free, are capable of love and community, and have an innate tendency to move toward their true destiny as the people of God. Now we shall consider the acts of God by which He implements His purpose in human history.

Implementation

The implementation of the divine purpose may be understood as a drama in two acts.

The first act is the series of God's actions beginning with Abraham and continuing through Jesus and the gift of the Spirit at Pentecost. It is not necessary to review these acts in detail, as they were spelled out in Part I. What is important is that we recognize that, throughout the story told in the Bible, God was acting to create a people who freely accept Him as God and who receive His love and who then respond by loving Him and others.

Three questions arise concerning the acts of God in the Bible. The first concerns what we are to make of God's actions and purpose before Abraham. The story of the Hebrews does not begin until Genesis 12; what then are we to think of Genesis 1—11? Since it is such a small part of the Bible, it is not absolutely necessary to fit it into our survey. And yet, in a limited way we can see how it fits. For even before God called Abraham, God's purpose was evident. We shall observe three examples of this.

First, in Eden, God was concerned that Adam and Eve be together. They were the first community, a community of two persons. The divine concern about their being a community is evident in the words, "It is not good that the man should be alone" (Gen. 2:18). God's purpose was that Adam and Eve be His people, but they chose instead to rebel, to follow the serpent's way.

The second example concerns Cain and Abel. Their story shows the failure of Cain to accept God as God—by offering improper worship —and the resultant loss of community as Cain killed Abel. God's purpose was the same.

The third example is the story of Noah. It is an awesome story. As told in Genesis 6—10, it seems to say that at one point in human history God came very close to scrapping His project! It is a very humbling thing to remember that God has freely chosen His purpose and that He continues to carry it out because He is a God of grace, not because He is under some obligation or has some need to do so.

So we conclude that even before Abraham, God's purpose was to create a people for Himself.

The second question concerns the nature of God's acts in history. Are all the acts of God miracles? The answer to the question depends on how the word *miracle* is understood. In a wide sense of the word *miracle,* all God's acts in history are miracles because they are God's acts.

In a more narrow sense of the word, a miracle is an intervention in nature. It is an act of God which occurs outside of or contrary to the normal routines of nature. For example, the normal routine of nature is that when people die they remain dead. Thus the resurrection of Christ was a miracle not only in the broad, general sense but in the more narrow sense as well.

God's acts in history include both miraculous and nonmiraculous events. Thus, the death of Christ was an act of God, nonmiraculous in the sense that men who are crucified naturally die. And Christ's resurrection was a miraculous act of God in the sense that ordinarily dead men do not rise from the dead.

The biblical outlook on miracles is interesting. The Bible reports several dozen miracles, in three main clusters; the first group is related to Moses and the Exodus, the second to the prophetic work of Elijah and Elisha, and the third to Jesus and His followers. The Bible also reports miracles done by enemies of the Lord, for example, the miracles of Pharaoh's priests (Ex. 7:22).

The idea that God can do miracles is of course consistent with the idea that He is the Creator. So, likewise, is the idea that the natural world operates in an orderly routine. While the Jewish people did not talk about "natural law," they did know that nature is orderly and recognized interventions in the order when they occurred.

The Bible also contains warnings against an excessive emphasis on miracles. Jesus said that "an evil and adulterous generation seeketh after a sign" (Matt. 12:39) and refused to give any sign, that is, to perform a miracle. Asked by Herod to do a miracle, Jesus responded with a stony silence (see Luke 23:8-9). Paul also spoke disparagingly about Greeks who seek wisdom and Jews who seek a sign and declared that all they would get from him was the proclamation of the gospel (1 Cor. 1:22-23).

The one miracle which the Bible does emphasize is the resurrection of Christ. It alone is a part of the gospel, and upon the truth of it Christian faith depends.

Our final question concerning the nature of God's acts in history is, How do we recognize them? What is their identifying mark? The answer is that there is no identifying mark. The miraculous is not a mark, since, as we have seen, God's acts are not all miracles. Nor is there any other identifying mark.

How then can we know that God has acted? The answer is in two parts. Concerning the past, God equipped certain men to recognize His acts and to interpret them, and also He commissioned His people to preach His acts as interpreted by these men. In other words, the church has preached and continues to preach the acts of God as reported and interpreted by the prophets and apostles. We have heard this preaching and have accepted it.

Concerning God's acts in the present, the situation is rather different. We are open to God's acting in contemporary history, in the church, and in our lives because we know that He has acted in the past. We have no authority for saying that God no longer acts. We may presume that, since He was an agent in past historical acts, He continues to act in history.

What we can and do believe is that the revelation given in the Bible is sufficient for the needs of Christian faith. We do not have to have further revelations of a private nature in order to know about God and His purpose. If God chooses to continue to reveal Himself, we accept that gratefully, but we also accept the sufficiency of the Holy Scriptures.

Further, we recognize how difficult it is to interpret an act of God in the present. We therefore affirm God's acts today with less confidence than we do God's acts in the past. For past acts we have an authoritative interpretation which we do not have for God's present acts.

But in the end, Christians are very concerned about what God is doing in their world and in their lives. Interest in God's acts today is very high, and to that subject, which is act 2 in the drama of the implementation of the divine purpose, we now turn.

God's work did not end with the completion of the Bible. He is still active in His world and, in particular, among His people. A long list of His continuing activities might be drawn up. It would include guiding and empowering His church, convincing people of the truth of the gospel and attracting them to it, binding His people into a unity, giving gifts to equip His people for service, transforming His people into more loving persons, and so on. The list could be extended, and many items on the list could be expressed differently.

Three comments may be made about God's work today. First, He continues to work to fulfill the same purpose which we saw earlier, the creation of a community of persons. Second, God's work is always centered upon, and consistent with, His ultimate act in Jesus Christ. Third, His work in the present is utterly free; He may be doing things about which we know nothing.

We have spoken of God's acts of preparation for and implementation of His purpose. Now we shall briefly consider the completing of His work.

Consummation

Our knowledge of each of the three aspects of God's work differs. The past work of God is fulfilled. We know it as past, as history, through the authoritative interpretation of it in the Bible. The present work of God is still going on. We experience it ourselves, and we attempt to interpret it as best we can.

We "know" the future work of God in still another way. It is not a finished work interpreted for us or a present experience interpreted by us. It is a future work, and in that sense it does not exist—not yet. We know it, not as history or experience, but as hope.

Human beings lean into the future. A person with no hope for the future becomes paralyzed. It is essential to human existence that we have something to look forward to.

Christians are provided with hope by the promise of God. The God who created the heavens and the earth speaks to us of a new heaven and a new earth (Rev. 21). The God whose greatest act of love was His coming (*parousia* in Greek) into our world has promised another coming to complete the work He began. "We know that, when he shall appear, we shall be like him" (1 John 3:2). "Being confident of this very thing, that he which hath begun a good work in you will perform it until the day of Jesus Christ" (Phil. 1:6).

Grateful as we are for God's work in history and in our experience, we are led by the affirmation of the Bible and by the logic of that work to believe that God is going to do yet another work.

For our purpose here, the important thing to notice about the future acts of God is this: They will be done in such a way that God's purpose is fulfilled. In other words, God will act to complete the creation of a community of persons who freely accept Him as God and also receive His love into their hearts and who respond by loving Him with all their hearts and by loving others as themselves. I shall attempt now to describe that completion of God's purpose for which we hope. Since the most widely used description of the consummation of God's purpose is heaven, I shall attempt to spell out the nature of that consummation in terms of heaven.

In heaven, all persons will be free. They will not be bound by sin or ignorance or fear or any other enslaving power.

In heaven, all persons will live together as family. No one will be left out, not one will feel alienated, no one will be lonely. The community will be united.

In heaven, all persons will know God as God. His kingdom or rule over His people will be complete. He will be known and loved by all His people. He will be their God and they will be His people.

In heaven, everyone will be fully loved by God.

In heaven, everyone will love God with all their hearts and minds and souls and strength. No cloud will hide God's face. No sin will distort our vision of God.

In heaven, everyone will love everyone else as themselves. Mutual love and trust will characterize our existence. No one will be afraid, unhappy, confused, or selfish.

In many ways, the consummation of God's purpose is a mystery to us. There is much about it that we do not understand. But we know enough to hope for it and to live each day with the optimism and freedom which that hope gives. For that hope, optimism, and freedom, we may be thankful to God.

The principal things we have said about God's acts are these: First, He acts in ways that respect human freedom. The acts by which He prepared for His purpose included creating nature as a home for mankind and creating human beings as free, capable of participating in His purpose, and inclined toward His purpose. The acts by which He implements His purpose included His past work described and authoritatively interpreted in the Bible and His present work experienced by us and interpreted by us in light of the biblical revelation. And the act by which He will consummate His purpose is known to us as a hope which is founded upon the promise of the Bible, a hope that God will fulfill His purpose of creating a community of persons who accept Him as God, receive His love into their lives, and respond by loving Him with all their hearts and by loving their neighbors as themselves.

7

The Character of God

Our Theological Tradition

We have come now to the place in which we select some adjectives which are descriptive of God. At this point, the theological tradition has a great many suggestions to offer us, for the theologians have shown a special interest in drawing up lists of adjectives to characterize God.

The customary name for these is the attributes of God. Other names have included the perfections of God and the qualities of God.

Lists of God's attributes are often analytical in character. That is, theologians have listed the divine attributes in categories. One such analysis distinguishes the immanent and relative attributes of God. The immanent attributes are those which God has within himself, without reference to any relationship to His creation; an example is His omniscience, His knowledge of all things. The relative attributes are those which God does not have within Himself but only in relationship to His creation; an example is His mercy.

Another analysis of the attributes of God distinguishes His moral from His metaphysical attributes. An example of metaphysical attributes is God's omnipotence, or power. Power is morally neutral and may be used well or badly. An example of a moral attribute is God's righteousness.

Theologians who utilized the tradition concerning God's attributes often draw up long lists of these. Sometimes they arranged them in pairs such as love/holiness; and other times they simply listed them.

Usually an effort was made to provide a comprehensive statement about God's attributes.

While we all can be grateful for these efforts, we also need to be sensitive to their limitations.

First, no one can provide a complete list of God's attributes. In fact, we cannot provide a complete list of the attributes of a human being. If we give a list of divine attributes, we must be very selective and we must make no claims for completeness.

Second, a long list of attributes communicates unreality. This is unintentional, of course. But when the theologians listed thirty or forty attributes of God, the format served to suggest that God is not real. The procedure felt contrived.

This is not hard to understand. Imagine trying to describe a human being by listing forty qualities, carefully divided into categories, perhaps paired up in some manner. It is an entirely artificial procedure.

We sense the artificiality of it with reference to God also, and we instinctively feel that a God described in such a manner is somehow unreal.

How might we speak of God so as to avoid this artificiality?

First, we must frankly select what we say about God. That is what we do when we talk about people. We select the really important characteritics and do not attempt completeness. We say: "She is gorgeous" or "He is brilliant" or "They are kind" or "She is determined." Being selective is difficult, but it is necessary if we are to portray a person with any helpfulness and realism. The same is true in our portrait of God. We must have the courage to be selective in what we say.

Second, we must attempt to be representative. We must select those characteristics of God which are most important about Him. In particular, we must select those characteristics of God which are most helpful to us as we attempt to relate to God. We want to include what is most important about God for our faith and life. In order to do this well, we need wisdom.

A selective list of God's attributes will give us an impressionistic portrait of God. It will not be as precise as a photograph and certainly not as precise as a diagram! But it may be suggestive, leading us to appreciate God's character in a deeper and more meaningful way. And it has the advantage of being a natural procedure, and therefore one that has the ring of reality about it.

With this is mind, I want to suggest that we consider four qualities of God. They are His love and goodness and His wisdom and power. The two pairs correspond roughly to the distinction between moral and metaphysical attributes, but I do not want to press that very much.

Love and Goodness

Let us recall now what we are doing. In our construction of a verbal portrait of God, we began by saying that God is the Transcendent One. His purpose is to create a community. He acts to carry out that purpose.

Now we are asking what kind of a One God is. How should this One be described? What is His character?

And we begin by saying that He is loving and that He is good.

A deep religious and moral sense tells us that these qualities of God are very important. We cannot demonstrate this importance by rational proof or even by argument, but we intuitively feel and know that they matter very much. Some instinct tells us that a description of God which failed to make these qualities apparent would be profoundly flawed.

And yet, ultimately it is not because of our intuitive instinct that we believe that God is good and loving. Not at all. Our conviction that this is what God is like rests exactly where all our other convictions about God rest—on His self-disclosure.

Certainly it is not obvious as we look at our world that God is loving and good. Our world is filled with suffering. Often it seems pointless and undeserved. The universe seems indifferent to the agonies of human beings and beasts. Nature is red in tooth and claw.

Why then should we believe that God is good and loving? We believe it because that is what God has revealed to us about Himself.

We have repeatedly said in this book that God is free to reveal

Himself in whatever way He likes. We here call attention to two ways in which God has revealed His love and goodness.

First, the Bible contains direct affirmations of God's love and goodness. The words *good* and *love* are used of God, along with many related words such as *righteous, compassion, kind, gentle, grace,* and *mercy.*

An example of this is Psalm 100. The message of this popular song may be expressed in a series of short phrases: Praise the Lord/The Lord is God/He made us/We are his/Thank the Lord/He is good/His love is forever.

Affirmations of God's love and goodness are found throughout the Bible. For example, Paul's Letter to the Romans mentions both of these qualities of God. The righteousness of God is a major theme of that letter; often it refers to God's saving work as well as to God's character, as in Romans 3:21: "But now the righteousness of God without the law is manifested." The association of God's righteous character with His act of righteousness (salvation) is important. Both were concerns of Paul, as can be seen a few verses later when Paul referred to God as both "just, and the justifier" (v. 26).

Paul also spoke eloquently in Romans of love, as in the familiar words "I am persuaded, that neither death, nor life, nor angels, nor principalities, nor powers, nor things present, nor things to come, Nor height, nor depth, nor any other creature, shall be able to separate us from the love of God, which is in Christ Jesus our Lord" (Rom. 8:38-39). And this quality of God also is closely associated with God's action: "But God commendeth his love toward us, in that, while we were yet sinners, Christ died for us" (Rom. 5:8).

We see the same connection of personal chracteristics with action in John's writings. He wrote quite simply that "God is love" (1 John 4:8), but he quickly added, "He loved us, and sent his Son to be the propitiation for our sins" (v. 10).

The reason for the connection between the character of love and the acts of love is clear. Christians believe that love is fundamentally a matter of action rather than of words or emotions. It is difficult for our contemporaries to recognize this because, in our time, the widespread assumption is that love is basically a feeling which expresses itself principally in words. The biblical understanding is that love is a personal commitment which expresses itself in actions. "My little children, let us not love in word, neither in tongue; but in deed and in truth" (1 John 3:18). This is true of human love, and it is likewise true of God's love; it is real because it is expressed in actions. And because God's actions always are expressive of His love, we naturally conclude that love is characteristic of God.

We have arrived now at a second form of the revelation of God's love and goodness. The first form was verbal; we read of God's love and goodness in the Bible, as in Psalm 100. The second form is action. We see God's love and goodness in what He does.

By observing God's actions, writers of the Bible first learned of God's love and goodness. Led by the Spirit, they were able to interpret God's works as the work of One who was Himself good and loving, and they were able then to communicate those truths in their writings.

We too are able to see God's goodness and love in His actions. Indeed, we are invited to do so, as when John insisted, "Hereby perceive we the love of God, because he laid down his life for us" (1 John 3:16). Again, "In this was manifested the love of God toward us, because that God sent his only begotten Son into the world" (1 John 4:9).

John was, in effect, inviting us to consider Jesus and His sacrifice and to draw our own conclusions about what God is like. The inevitable conclusion is, of course, that God is love. The One who was crucifed for us, loves us. We can likewise conclude from the divine action in Christ that God is a good God, doing what is right, unimplicated in the failures of mankind, but still taking upon Himself the responsibility of rescuing us from our moral failure.

Two questions may be asked concerning God's goodness and love. One is quite down-to-earth and experiential. The other is highly abstract and logical.

The experiential question is this: Do we not observe events which we attribute to God, which suggest that God is loveless and even evil rather than loving and good? For example, natural disasters are very destructive, and we refer to them as "acts of God" in our insurance policies.

A longer response to this question will be given in chapter 9. For now, two things may be said. First, God does not do all the things which are attributed to Him. The assumption that a tragedy "must have been the will of God" often needs to be challenged; and when this interpretation stands, it needs to be interpreted carefully. Second, even if some events seem to suggest that God is not good and loving, still other acts, such as Christ and His cross, demonstrate unambiguously and decisively that God is good and loving. The God who gave up His life for His world cares—there is no mistaking that. And He who died to put us right can be depended on to do right Himself. That is a moral certainty. What we must do is to interpret other divine activities in the light of this ultimate act of God, this deepest revelation of His character as loving and good.

The second question which may be asked is a logical but difficult question. It is this: If God is the ultimate good, then He is the ultimate standard for all goodness and love; whatever then do we mean when we say that God is Himself good and loving? The problem is entirely a logical one: What standard do you use to measure the ultimate standard?

The same question can be expressed the other way around. Suppose God tortured people for no reason; would that then mean that torture is good and loving since God is the standard of love and goodness?

Because the problem is entirely abstract, it does not interest all Christians, but some are troubled by it. It seems to me to be important, and it also seems to me to be answerable in part.

What is helpful is for us to realize that the character of all our language about God is analogical. That is, all of our words get their basic meanings from the mundane, created world. When we then use these words to speak of the One who transcends the mundane world, we are using them in a special way. We use them of God very seriously and very truthfully, but we do not use them in exactly the same way we use them of the world.

For example, we say that God is our Heavenly Father. This is a serious use of the word *father,* a true use. But it also is a special use, for God is not Father in exactly the same sense that our earthly fathers are. One obvious example of a difference is that, whereas we could have no earthly father unless we had an earthly mother, we have a Heavenly Father but no heavenly mother.

That is how we must understand the qualities of love and goodness in God. They are analogies. For example, we know the difference between a true, good friend and a person who pretends to be a friend but really dislikes us. When we say that God is good we mean that He is like a true friend, not a person who only pretends to be our friend. Of course, this is an analogy, and God's goodness vastly exceeds the goodness of even our best friends; but it is a true analogy, for God is like a good friend; He certainly is not like a person who merely pretends to care about us.

The same thing is true of God's love. It is an analogy, a very true and important one, for understanding God. For example, we all recognize the difference between a father who loves his son and is interested in him and a father who wishes he did not have a son and does not like his son at all. God, we say, is like the first father. He loves us. Of course, His love goes far beyond the love of an earthly father; we recognize the limitations of our language. But our language is true as far as it goes. It is true and important to say that God is loving.

Our question was, If God is the standard, then have we asserted anything when we say that God is loving and good? The answer is that we have. It is not that we have access to an eternal standard outside of God to which He must measure up. Not at all. Rather, we have learned from our experience of life the difference between good and bad people, between loving and unloving people. Our definitions of these may be only rough ones, and our experiences are limited, but we do most certainly recognize the difference And in light of these recognitions, we look at Jesus and His sacrifice and say, Now that is what love is really like! That is what goodness is really like!

Let us now express this in another way. Let us suppose that a mother wants to teach her child about right and wrong. What types of teaching are available? What forms of expressions may she use? Several are available. I shall mention three.

First, she may express her teaching in commands. For example, she may say to her child, "Do not be selfish."

Second, she may express her teaching in terms of abstract values. She may lead her child to understand the meaning of the value called "generosity." It is in terms of such values that we are speaking when we say that God is good and loving. Goodness and love are values.

Third, the mother may express her teaching by how she lives. She may live according to her own command, "Do not be selfish." She may embody in her life the values of generosity. She may act generously and unselfishly.

We believe that God lives out the values of love and goodness. He acts lovingly and in a good way. In Jesus Christ, we see these divine qualities incarnated, and we know that God is love.

We have been attempting to select the best adjectives for describing the Transcendent One, and we have used *loving* and *good*. We believe that God's actions cry out for these two descriptions, especially His act in Christ. We also believe that God's purpose of creating a people of His own is a loving, good purpose. We find it incomprehensible that anyone could know the truth of the cross and think otherwise of God. And we know of no qualities of God which the life and ministry of Jesus press upon us more urgently than these two.

Now we shall look at two other qualities of God which, so far from being revealed by the cross, seem actually to be challenged by the cross.

Wisdom and Power

God's creative, rather than His redemptive, activity presses upon us the importance of His power and wisdom. The logic is quite straightforward. The One who created and controls this large, complex universe must have a knowledge and wisdom of awesome proportions. Further, He must have power beyond the imagining of most of us.

This is all true and should be accepted. But it is not quite that simple.

First, we need to recognize here once again the analogical character of our language. When we say that God is powerful, we are distinguishing between a weak, ineffectual person and a strong, achieving person. We are saying that God is more like the second than the first, though of course God's power exceeds the power of any human person. The doctrine of creation leads us to that conclusion.

Further, when we say that God is wise, we are distinguishing between an uninformed, foolish person and an intelligent, thoughtful, informed person; and we are saying that God is more like the second than the first, though we recognize that God's wisdom exceeds all human wisdom. The doctrine of creation leads us to that conclusion.

Second, we must remind ourselves that the qualities of power and wisdom apply to God as personal. We have spoken of His nature as both unlike us, transcendent, and as like us, personal. God is the Transcendent One. And this Transcendent One is powerful and wise.

In other words, God's power is more like the power of a person than like the power of electricity, radioactivity, or gravity. And God's wisdom is more like the wisdom of a person than like the information stored in a bank of computers.

We did not need a reminder of this when we spoke of love and goodness, for these qualities are moral and exist only in persons. But power and wisdom (or knowledge) are not moral, and they exist outside of persons. So we must remember that they are qualities of a personal God, not of an abstraction.

Third, power and wisdom are morally neutral. They can be put in the service of good or of evil, of love or of hatred.

It is obvious that in God, power and wisdom are always in the service of love and goodness. This is a very important fact.

But it leads us to an even more important fact and a really astonishing one. Because God's power and wisdom are always exercised in the service of His love and goodness, they are transformed. In other words, since God is entirely good and loving, He uses His power and wisdom in ways that are different than we might have supposed that He would.

How are God's power and wisdom revealed to us? We began on the assumption that they are revealed in creation, and so they are. But we know that creation is not God's deepest and most complete self-disclosure. The ultimate revelation of God was given in Christ rather than in creation. That is true of God's love and goodness; the ultimate revelation of these was given in the cross and resurrection. Likewise, the ultimate revelation of God's power and wisdom was given in Christ, in His cross and resurrection.

And that means that God does not always use His power as raw power or His wisdom as raw knowledge. He accommodates himself to the human situation. He deploys His power and wisdom in a way that is appropriate for His purpose of creating a people who freely accept Him and His love.

What does this involve? In Christ, it involved the acceptance of limitations upon His power and knowledge. The sacrifice of Christ is by all the usual human standards an example of weakness rather than of strength and of foolishness rather than of wisdom. The world assumes that the strong survive and the weak perish, and Christ perished. The world believes that the wise win and the foolish lose, and Christ lost. To die on the cross was weak and foolish as the world counts things. But "the foolishness of God is wiser than men; and the weakness of God is stronger than men" (1 Cor. 1:25).

What we have here is the transvaluation of values. By being weak and by dying, Christ is strong. By being foolish and giving up His life, Christ is wise.

This is all mysterious if we try to get it rationally. It helps a little to say that God used His (raw) power to raise Christ, and so He did. But that was not exactly Paul's point. Paul was pointing out that precisely in the weakness of death, Christ was strong; He was strong not only in the resurrection but in the death itself. The same is true of the foolishness of sacrificing Himself; it is the sacrifice itself, not only the resurrection, that is wise.

This transvaluation of values is found elsewhere in Christ's life and work, and other biblical writers spoke of it. For example, it is precisely by being the servant of others that Christ is the Lord (see Mark 10:44-45). Again, John used a curious phrase of Jesus several times; He spoke of Jesus being "lifted up." The phrase is ambiguous. It refers both to Christ being crucified (lifted upon on a cross) and to His being glorified (lifted up in the sense of exalted; see, for example, John 3:14-16). The unusual thing is that it is precisely in the humiliation of the cross that the glory is most clearly seen.

How are we to understand all this? We cannot get it by merely rational thinking. It is not just a mystery for our minds to puzzle out.

It is rather got by our hearts. We learn it by experience. It is given to us precisely as a revelation, as we take seriously the gospel that Christ died for our sins and rose again (1 Cor. 15:1-7).

Let us remind ourselves that we are free persons. We live in a society where slavery is considered immoral and illegal. We live in a democracy where women and men are all free. No one puts a yoke on our necks or shackles our wrists. We are truly independent.

And yet, we free people have voluntarily bowed our knees to God. We have accepted him as our Master, and we have committed ourselves to be His servants, to do His will. We have done this freely. He did not force it on us.

What led us to do this? By what message were we free persons persuaded to yield our lives to God? Was it the message of His power in creation? It was not. Was it the message of His wisdom in creation? It was not. What then won our loyalty and our allegiance?

It was the message of the cross. The One who served us, Jesus, led us to respond by giving ourselves to be His servants. We did this freely and enthusiastically.

And so, for us, the ultimate wisdom of God is not what we know about how complex a world God created. His ultimate wisdom is this: He accepted limitations in His knowledge and did what all the world believes is foolish in order to elicit from us a free response of love and trust and gratitude. And God's ultimate power for us is this: He accepted limitations in His power and did what all the world believes is weak in order to elicit from us a free response of love and gratitude and trust.

The weakness of the cross is the power of God by which His purpose of creating a community of free persons is ultimately carried out, and the foolishness of the cross is the wisdom of God by which His purpose of creating a community of free persons is ultimately carried out. Since God has by the cross dislodged us from the world and led us voluntarily to live under his rule or kingdom, we must confess with Paul that "the foolishness of God is wiser than men; and the weakness of God is stronger than men" (1 Cor. 1:25).

You Can Trust This God

We have come now to the conclusion of our constructive doctrinal portrait of God. I began by suggesting that God is personal and transcendent; He is the Transcendent One. I then stated that His purpose is to create a family of free persons who accept Him as God, receive His love into their lives, and learn to love Him with all their hearts and to love their neighbors as themselves. Next we pointed out that God acts to carry out this purpose. He acted in a preparatory way by creating the world and the human beings in it; He acted to implement His purpose by His mighty deeds among the Jewish people, especially Jesus, and also by the work which He continues to do today; and He will act to consummate the work He has begun, in the final day, in heaven. All of these acts are consistent with His purpose of creating a free covenant community. Finally, I have said that God is good and loving and that He is wise and powerful. I suggested that God accommodates His wisdom and power to us so that He can elicit from us a free response of love and trust.

I close Part II with two observations. First, a God such as I have described, a God such as is revealed in the Bible and especially in Christ, is an utterly trustworthy God. His trustworthiness is seen in His gracious purpose; it is made possible by the fact that He is both personal and transcendent; it is confirmed by His actions; and it is exemplified in His character as good, loving, powerful, and wise, especially when His power and wisdom are understood as being always in the service of His love and goodness.

Many people do not believe in God, do not trust. I shall say more about belief and unbelief in Part III. For now, the important thing is that everything in our portrait of God supports the idea that God may be trusted to be our Friend our God, our Father, our Savior.

Further, the purpose of our effort to construct a verbal portrait of God was not merely to possess the portrait. Our purpose was to understand and appreciate God better. We wanted to understand in order to relate to God as best we can.

Traditionally Christians have spoken of relating to God in terms of faith, hope, and love. Only as we are willing to relate to God in these ways will our verbal portrait have been of serious value to us as Christians.

Part III
Relational

Christians relate to God in many ways. For example, they worship, pray, sing, and are morally obedient to God. There is no one way to describe how Christians respond to God.

One traditional description of how Christians relate to God is in terms of faith, hope, and love. Paul mentioned these three early in his first letter (see 1 Thess. 1:3), and in 1 Corinthians he wrote, "Now abideth faith, hope, [love], these three" (13:13). We will follow this traditional pattern of faith, hope, and love as we explore how Christians today relate to God.

Each of these three themes has a special meaning in the modern world.

The special meaning of faith derives from the fact that our world today contains widespread unbelief. What leads us Christians to go on believing in God when so many in our world do not?

The special meaning of hope arises from the massive suffering of people in the twentieth century and from the challenge which that suffering offers to Christianity. How do we continue to hope when things look so hopeless?

The special meaning of love arises from our recognition that in some mysterious way God is eternally loving and being loved and that this is true even apart from His creation. We need to explore the doctrine of the Trinity to understand how this can be so and to appreciate the love of God in our lives.

We now turn to each of these themes.

8
Faith: God and Unbelief

Our Modern Situation

Christian faith is personal trust in God as He has revealed himself in Jesus Christ, to be our Friend, our Father, our Savior, and our God. The closest analogues for this faith are the trust which children have in their parents and the trust which happily married persons have in their spouses.

Understood in this way, faith has never been easy. The story of the Bible is the story of persons who were called to have personal faith in God but often failed to have it either because they stubbornly refused or because they found life so filled with ambiguity that it was difficult to really trust in God.

Nevertheless, people in the past had one factor which supported their faith which is lacking in our modern situation. This was the fact that everyone in the ancient world had a religious view of life. The universal acceptance of a supernatural or religious view of life supported the Hebrews and the Christians in their faith in God. In the world of the first century, for example, there were many religions and many philosophies, but all were committed to a supernatural understanding of life. Christianity had to make its way against these alternative religious views, but it did not have to fight against vast numbers of people who presupposed that religion was irrelevant nonsense. The only question to be answered was, Which religion?

And in the medieval period in Europe, even that question was almost put to rest. Europe was Christendom. True, Christians knew about the existence of Jews and Moslems, but their beliefs were not serious options for the vast majority of people living in Europe. The only belief system with any real social support was the Christian.

Of course, individuals still had to struggle to put personal faith in Christ, to be loyal and obedient. But in those earlier ages, they always had the social support that came from knowing that, for all practical purposes, everyone agreed that Christianity was true and important.

Today, all this has changed. What is characteristic of our modern age is that the widespread social support for religion has been withdrawn. It is no longer the case that practically everyone agrees that the Christian belief system is true. On the contrary, the official public view toward religion is now neutral. In Europe and North America and in other countries which are highly developed scientifically and technologically, the official attitude toward religion is one of benign neglect.

A nonreligious understanding of life is now available to all who grow up in these countries. Occasionally a nonreligious interpretation of life is articulated. For example, some people have spelled out the meaning of life as understood in naturalistic and evolutionary terms. Here is how the philosopher Bertrand Russell put it:

> That man is the product of causes which had no prevision of the end they were achieving; that his origin, his growth, his hopes and fears, his loves and his beliefs, are but the outcome of accidental collocations of atoms; that no fire, no heroism, no intensity of thought and feeling, can preserve an individual life beyond the grave; that all the labors of the ages, all the devotion, all the inspiration, all the noonday brightness of human genius, are destined to extinction in the vast death of the solar system, and that the whole temple of man's achievement must inevitably be buried beneath the debris of a universe in ruins—all these things, if not quite beyond dispute, are yet so nearly certain that no philosophy which rejects them can hope to stand. Only within the scaffolding of these truths, only on the firm foundation of unyielding despair, can the soul's habitation henceforth be safely built.[1]

Another nonreligious view of life is that of Marxism or Communism. Clearly Communism is intended by some intellectuals to be a comprehensive interpretation of human life and history. It describes the human dilemma as alienation resulting from an unjust distribution of wealth, and it understands salvation to be the creation of a society in which all members share equally in all the wealth. It resists traditional religion as a distraction from what really matters, which is wealth, and even as a hindrance to the achievement of the more just society; religion is an opiate which drugs the masses of the people and so prevents them from overthrowing the unjust rulers of society. Marxism's interpretation of history is that history is moving dialectically toward socialism. That is, the absolutely inevitable outcome of history is the establishment of a worldwide Communist system.

Another interpretation of life is the hedonistic. This understanding of life rests on the agnostic assumption that life is an inexplicable mystery, and it concludes that the only sensible goal in life is pleasure. Pleasure may be sensual, as in the philosophy of sexually explicit magazines, or more intellectual and refined, but in either case the point of life is to seize as much personal pleasure out of life as possible. The only moral rule which matters is not to be cruel toward others; apart from that, anything goes. In this belief system, the only ultimate reality is the individual and his pleasure.

These three alternatives are offered to people in the modern Western world. But I doubt if they are very widely accepted. Millions of people have not consciously accepted either a religious belief system or any one of these three. They live from day to day without a conscious commitment to any system of beliefs. They feel that they can get along quite well without any of these. They have tactics for coping with what life sends to them each day, but they have no overall strategy for grappling with the ultimate question of the meaning of their lives. Of course, such an attitude is itself nonreligious.

Occasionally, therefore, a nonreligious view is articulated, but far more often it is simply presupposed.

And the important thing to notice is this: In modern society, this nonreligious understanding of life is never officially challenged. Of course, it is always being challenged by the churches; that is not what I mean. I mean that it is never challenged in public life, officially.

In particular, both our American government and our media are religiously neutral. Neither offers a serious corrective to the nonreligious interpretations of life. Our government is tolerant of all religions and of none. That is what is meant by religious liberty. And our television, movies, songs, and books offer us portrayals of life being lived without benefit of religious faith. When a novelist, such as Graham Green, John Updike, or Walker Percy, writes a book which suggests that religious faith is an important matter, he is instantly recognized as being out of the mainstream of contemporary literature.

An outsider might assume that Christians would be deeply opposed to the religious neutrality of the government and the media. The truth is the opposite. Our religious forebears first proposed the then astonishing idea that religious liberty should be tried. The United States was the first country to be launched without an official state religion to act as a cement to hold its people together. It was a daring experiment; no one really knew if it were possible for a country with religious pluralism to hold together. We believe that the history of the United States demonstrates that religious pluralism does not shatter the unity of a country; a country can unite around its commitment to religious liberty.

We Christians think that it is wonderful that this modern experiment has worked. We favor allowing, or rather encouraging, people to think for themselves. We do not want a general censorship of the media, and we resist calling upon government and the media to underwrite the religious enterprise. We have no desire to turn America into a religious state, such as Iran has been transformed into with its censorship, loss of freedom, and repression.

So in Europe and North America, the official position of the government and the media is neutrality toward religion, and we who are Christians support this.

On the other hand, the result is that millions of people are growing up in a country in which a nonreligious view of life is socially acceptable. What happens to faith in this unique modern situation?

We might suppose that it would result in the death of religion. But that is not what has happened. Religion continues to survive in

Europe and to flourish in America, especially in the United States which is religiously the most neutral country of all. We are not a secular people, though many suppose that we are; we are a religious people.

However, religion is now perceived by many people in an unusual way. It is understood as a private matter. In the United States, for example, religion is treated by the government and the media, and following them by many people, as a kind of hobby, harmless and even nice for those who happen to go in for that sort of thing. It is understood as a nonrational activity, like snorkeling or baseball or marriage; religion exists for the same reason that these other things do, that some people just choose to practice it. It is tolerated, but not taken seriously. Its truth claims are dismissed as excessive and unwarranted. Theologian David Tracy has named this the privatization of religious faith.

Clearly we Christians cannot be content with this benign neglect. We want to insist that our faith is not an innocent hobby for those who just happen to be interested, but the only fulfillment of the deepest need of all human beings. How then should we respond to the privatization of religion?

The churches have, in fact, tended to respond in one of three ways. First, some Christians have revised their faith to fit the nonreligious presuppositions of our modern world. They have taken the sacred out of Christianity, making it into a secular faith.

This solution is unsatisfying. For one thing, it does not seem to be intellectually responsible to transform a supernaturalist understanding of life into a naturalistic one. For another thing, it is difficult to see why anyone would want the revised edition. It would be the self-liquidation of the Christian faith. We do not need to go to church to get a nonreligious view of life; we can get that on the television news.

Second, some Christians simply attempt to cut themselves off from the world and its religious neutrality and thus resist the stress which modernity puts on faith. In effect, they build a religious ghetto and live in it.

This is a more satisfying solution. In a sense, all Christians must live in a ghetto. That is, they must from time to time withdraw from the religiously neutral world and share in the common life of the community of faith. They must have their faith nourished by participating in the fellowship of common belief.

But as a complete answer this also is unsatisfying. It is one thing to withdraw into the fellowship of faith occasionally, but quite another to stay there permanently. Most Christians are required by their work and by other factors to participate in the religiously neutral world. Each time we watch television, ride on public transportation, attend a public school, visit our doctor, or go shopping, we engage the world to some extent. It is profoundly disquieting to function with faith in God while we are in church and then go out into the world and function as though God were irrelevant.

A third possibility presents itself to those who do not want the kind of intellectual schizophrenia just described. It is to locate traces of the supernatural in the religiously neutral world. If we can see hints of the reality of God within the nonreligious world, then we can understand faith as a following up on a vital dimension of common human experience, a dimension which is simply being overlooked or ignored by the world at large.

It is this alternative which I intend to follow. I believe that, in addition to the saving revelation which God has given in Christ and in the Bible, He also has given a more general revelation of Himself in the world which He created. This general revelation is deep in the hearts of human beings. The officially religiously neutral world still carries traces of God's reality, and I want now to look briefly at some of them.

A Hypothesis

Human beings are driven by a longing to find an ultimate meaning for their lives. They search for some purpose which transcends their own limited goals. They look for some order underlying the apparent chaos of life and history.

Some people are very articulate about this. Traditionally the way to articulate it was in religious terms. Other people are not so articulate. They may experience the drive for order as an anxiety which has no specific source or as an intellectual quest to see a pattern in things, or they may compulsively create order within the limited areas which are under their control, such as their homes.

In this quest human beings are never fully satisfied. They search for an ultimate truth which will integrate all the partial truths, an ultimate beauty which will ground all the finite, beautiful objects.

We sense this quest behind some of the powerful symbols by which human beings have understood their lives. For centuries a nearly universal symbol for human life has been a journey. Life is like a trip, and it has a destination (or destiny). The symbol of a journey is found in *The Odessey,* in *The Aeneid,* and in *Huckleberry Finn.* Why do people persistently think of life as like a journey? Why do they not accept it as a meaningless meandering, a wandering with no destination? The symbol of the journey is a trace of God's revelation which lingers on in the collective unconscious of people even in our religiously neutral world.

Another example of the need to find order is the way in which unreligious persons assure their children that life is good and is worth living. Here is an example from Peter Berger's very excellent book, *A Rumor of Angels.*

Consider the most ordinary, and probably most fundamental, of all— the ordering gesture by which a mother reassures her anxious child.

A child wakes up in the night, perhaps from a bad dream, and finds himself surrounded by darkness, alone, beset by nameless threats. At such a moment the contours of trusted reality are blurred or invisible, and in the terror of incipient chaos the child cries out for his mother. It is hardly an exaggeration to say that, at this moment, the mother is being invoked as a high priestess of protective order. It is she (and, in many cases, she alone) who has the power to banish the chaos and to restore the benign shape of the world. And, of course, any good mother will do just that. She will take the child and cradle him. . . . She will turn on a lamp, perhaps, which will encircle the scene with a warm glow of reassuring light. She will speak or sing to the child, and the content of this communication will invariably be the same—"Don't be afraid—everything is in order, everything is all right." If all goes well, the child will be reassured, his trust in reality recovered, and in this trust he will return to sleep.

All this, of course, belongs to the most routine experiences of life and does not depend upon any religious preconceptions. Yet this common scene raises a far from ordinary question, which immediately introduces a religious dimension: *Is the mother lying to the child?* The answer, in the most profound sense, can be "no" only if there is some truth in the religious interpretation of human existence. Conversely, if the natural is the only reality there is, the mother is lying to the child—lying out of love, to be sure, and obviously not lying to the extent that her reassurance is grounded in the fact of this love—but, in the final analysis, lying all the same. Why? *Because the reassurance, transcending the immediately present two individuals and their situation, implies a statement about reality as such.*[2]

In our effort to understand our lives as ordered and patterned, we are perfectly entitled to choose any kind of clue we want to make sense of things. Thus we could theoretically say that the ultimate explanation of things is found in the lower reaches of human experience. But something tells us that this is a mistake, that it is unreasonable to assume that the interaction of material forces could result in human existence. On the principle that a river cannot rise higher than its source, we are led to think that human life is explained satisfactorily only if it has a source greater than itself.

So we naturally turn to the highest reaches of our experience as we search for a pattern in life. The highest realities we experience are personal realities, with their intelligence, freedom, unselfish love, and other personal and moral qualities. The existence of some ultimate personal Being seems to be the only sufficient source for our lives. And if there were such a One, that would explain why we long for an ultimate reality; we are being drawn to Him. Further, that would mean that our longing can be ultimately fulfilled. Further, the existence of such a One would mean that human life is ultimately worth living; this conviction, by which we live each day, would be grounded in ultimate reality.

Objections to the Hypothesis

I am suggesting that our natural longings for order, sense, meaning, and purpose are traces of revelation of God still to be found in unreligious people, even in a religiously neutral society such as ours. This is not an argument; it is an observation which suggests that deep down we all instinctively resist the idea that life is "a tale, Told by an idiot, full of sound and fury, Signifying nothing."

Several objections could be offered to our hypothesis. First, it might be denied that people long for an ultimate explanation. It may be true that some people lack these longings. Apparently, however, most people have them. Not only has religion been a nearly universal phenomenon but many people today who are not religious confess that they share in the longing. Even if a few people had no such sense of longing, would they not be the exceptions that prove the rule? In our world there are a few people who are color blind, but that does not mean that those of us who see colors are imagining them; color blind people are the exception that proves the rule, which is that color is real and the vision of most of us is not deceiving us in this regard. It seems unreasonable that the existence of a few people who feel no longings for an ultimate order and purpose should lead us to ignore all the traces of this in all the rest of the world.

Second, it could be objected that nonreligious interpretations of the longing are available, and this is certainly true. For many people today the most convincing way to interpret the religious longings of people would be in psychological terms. Thus Sigmund Freud, in *The Future of an Illusion,* argued that the idea of God is a projection based on human need; when children are small, they learn to depend on their powerful fathers; as they grow older, they naturally (but mistakenly) come to believe in a Heavenly Father.

This is an interesting observation. But does that prove that religious longings are mistaken? It is one thing to say that our longing is a projection of childish needs, and quite another to say that it is nothing but such a projection. We are entitled to ask why it is that we human beings project a Heavenly Father. Why do we long for an ultimate meaning? Could it be that we were created by a God who made us so that we would project a Heavenly Father whom we need?

A third objection to the idea that our longing for meaning is a trace of divine revelation is simply to affirm that, though the longing is real and should not be explained away in psychological or any other terms, still it is a longing that must forever remain unfulfilled. The idea here is that we do seek after One who gives meaning, but He does not exist and our longing for Him does not lead us toward reality. It is all a mistake, a kind of cruel cosmic joke on us.

Theoretically this too is possible. But it would be very odd if it were the case. It would be as if people were created with a thirst for knowledge but there were no such thing as knowledge. It would be as if people were created with a sex drive but there were no such thing as sex. Theoretically it is possible, but it is not very convincing.

I have been suggesting that the human longings for meaning and purpose are traces of divine self-revelations to be found in all people, even in our religiously neutral world. These traces lead us to a hypothesis: The simplest and most reasonable explanation of this longing is that there is such a meaning and purpose for human life because there is One who created us all for a purpose and that we find our own true destiny by participating in His purpose for us.

The hypothesis is an attractive one. It has about it an elegant simplicity. It makes sense of our human experience. But is it believable? Do we have any way of confirming it?

We can put the same question another way. If it were the case that a personal One created our world and placed in our hearts these longings for meaning and purpose, and if He were like our highest experiences such as unselfish love, would it be too farfetched to suppose that He might communicate with us? Might He not reveal Himself and His purpose to us? Would it be too much to hope that somehow, somewhere, we might be given a clear and convincing revelation of this One, a revelation which would in effect confirm the hypothesis we constructed from the traces of God which we found in our lives?

Confirming the Hypothesis

In order to locate such a full revelation to confirm our hypothesis, it is necessary for us to turn away from the religiously neutral world to the world of religion. Within the lives of unreligious people we cannot find a revelation which is sufficient and clear enough to confirm the hypothesis.

When we turn to the world of religion, many options are open to us. The various world religions offer to us their doctrines, practices, founders, holy books, and moral systems. The only way to deal fully with them would be to consider them one by one.

That is not possible in this book. But I can suggest that attention be given to Jesus. For we believe that He is God's ultimate self-revelation. By His teachings, His life, His passion, and His resurrection, He reveals to us a God of goodness and love. He confirms the hypothesis which I constructed, that there is One whose existence grounds our conviction that life is meaningful, who embodies the highest values we experience, whose purpose offers an explanation for our longings for meaning and order. He makes it believable that God is love.

The appeal to Jesus is not, of course, a knock-down argument. Jesus does not prove God's love in such a way that only an irrational person can miss it. Not at all. During His own lifetime, many of His contemporaries failed to recognize the truth which was revealed in Jesus. Today many still do.

But the opposite is also true. Many of us have heard about Jesus and have concluded that our deepest longings are grounded in reality. There is a God of love and goodness who gives our lives an ultimate meaning.

In Jesus, we have a historical reality which has a strong claim to be an authentic revelation of God, a revelation which confirms our hypothesis that the existence of a Transcendent One accounts for our deepest longings.

Jesus makes our hypothesis reasonable. For many of us, He is the decisive factor. In the midst of life with all its ambiguities, it is Jesus who really makes faith possible for us. We freely believe in God because of Him.

Reasons and Causes

Now I want to be very clear about what I have been doing. I have not been attempting to describe how people come to faith. Rather I have been attempting to show that faith is a reasonable response to the divine revelation given in Jesus, in view of the hypothesis which we constructed out of the traces of revelation given in human existence.

Here we must distinguish between the reasons of faith and the causes of faith. The reasonableness of faith is located, I believe, in some such structure as I have described.

The causes of faith are quite another matter. They differ from person to person. Each person who has faith could trace out the causes which led him to that position. These would include the movements in his heart, the influence of persons in his life, and so on. In effect, he would be writing a spiritual autobiography.

For most people, there is not a very extensive coincidence between the reasons and the causes of faith. Occasionally one hears about a Christian who was led to faith by reasons, but this is rare. One such person was C. S. Lewis, and he has told his story in his autobiography, *Surprised by Joy.*

Our goal in all of this is not to attempt to argue for faith. I have spoken of traces of God and of a hypothesis and of a confirmation which is reasonable but not intellectually coercive. I have not spoken of a proof or of a knock-down argument.

What I have attempted to do is to show that faith is not restricted to an entirely private religious experience. It is a following up on traces of God which are deeply embedded in all human existence. It is an effort to think about the ultimate questions which cry out for our attention even though we live in a world which officially overlooks or ignores them.

I have further suggested that traces of divine self-revelation continue to exist even in very nonreligious people. They have not been eradicated; whether they ever will be, we do not know, but they are present now.

Further, I have constructed a hypothesis out of the traces of God. I am not forced to do this, of course, but it seems a reasonable procedure; we are accustomed to constructing hypotheses to account for other things we experience. We admit that other hypotheses than God could be proposed, but they do not seem to account for our longings as well as this one.

I further suggested that if this hypothesis were true, it would not be out of the question that God might give us a revelation sufficient to confirm to us what our own longings lead us to suspect. Such a revelation would necessarily be found in the religious rather than in the nonreligious world. While many candidates are available, Jesus has a special claim to our attention. And as we consider Him, we conclude that He does indeed confirm for us the hypothesis that behind our lives and our world is a God of love and goodness.

This, then, is how we continue to have religious faith even though we are living in a world which is officially neutral toward religion. We believe that in seeing God's revelation in Jesus, we are seeing the ultimate expression of what is expressed partially and fitfully in the human longing for meaning and purpose. Society may no longer provide us with official support for religious faith, but it continues, unintentionally of course, to provide us with traces of God. Taken together with Jesus' revelation, that is enough for us.

Notes

1. Bertrand Russell, *Why I Am Not a Christian,* p. 107.
2. Peter Berger, *A Rumor of Angels,* pp. 54-55.

9

Hope: God and Suffering

The Human Problem

All human beings suffer. All experience physical pain and personal suffering. Pain and suffering are not distributed to everyone in equal amounts, of course; some suffer terribly, beyond what many of us are able to comprehend; but no one escapes suffering.

The Bible contains many references to human suffering. The psalmist articulated the pain which we all feel. "My soul is full of troubles" (Ps. 88:3). Job could not understand why he suffered as he did. Jesus spoke of people killed in an accident at Siloam (Luke 13:1-4) and offered no explanation of their deaths, and he provided no interpretation of the cause of a man's blindness (John 9:1-7). He himself cried from His cross, "My God, my God, why hast thou forsaken me?" but no response came from God (Matt. 27:46).

Though our world is full of beautiful and wonderful things, and though we have many good experiences in our lives, no careful observer of life can fail to notice that the biblical realism about suffering is warranted. The cries of those who suffer rise from every corner of the earth in an uninterrupted chorus of agony. Natural disasters, physical and mental decay, crippling accidents, debilitating diseases, and violence are the lot of humankind.

Suffering is a universal human problem. It also is the most profound religious problem.

A Religious Problem

Suffering is a problem for many religions, perhaps for all. But it takes a special form in the Jewish-Christian religious tradition.

Our tradition, as we have seen, is that there is one and only one true and living God. He is good and loving, and He is wise and powerful. But if He is like this, then why do human beings suffer so much? For if God is good and loving, then He must want to prevent suffering; and if He is wise and powerful, then He must be able to prevent suffering; why then does suffering continue?

Suffering is the most serious challenge to our understanding of God. The challenge is both a logical one, as stated above, and an experiential one: How can we go on believing in God in view of all this suffering?

In Christian history, men such as Paul, Augustine, and Luther were troubled by the question: How can I, a sinner, be justified before God? For many modern people, things are reversed, and the question which cries out for an answer is: How can God, who is supposed to be good and loving and wise and powerful, be justified in people's eyes in light of all the suffering in our world? As C. S. Lewis expressed, today it seems that it is God who is in the dock, that is, on trial.[1]

This is not to suggest that it is only in our own time that suffering has become a hindrance to faith. On the contrary. That is precisely the theme of Job, for example. But today the acuteness of the problem is felt by many people. Perhaps in part this is a result of the magnitude of suffering in our time; perhaps in part it is a result of a general willingness of many modern people to ask tough questions rather than to meekly ignore them. In any case, the problem is widely felt.

Theodicy

Over the centuries many Christians have proposed solutions to the problem of suffering. Such proposals are called theodicies. The word *theodicy* is from two Greek words, *theos* (God) and *dike* (righteous or just). A theodicy is an effort to show that even though suffering occurs God is righteous. The best-known definition of a theodicy is a phrase

which John Milton used to state his purpose in writing *Paradise Lost;*
he intended "to justify the ways of God to man." The term *theodicy*
was coined by Gottfried Leibniz, a seventeenth-century philosopher.

Theodicies have taken many forms. Some actually have proposed
that we revise our understanding of God's nature so as to accommo-
date the reality and magnitude of suffering. A contemporary theologian, Fredcrick Sontag, has suggested that God is not entirely good,
that he has a shadow side to His personality, and that this explains
why He has not eliminated suffering from the earth.[2] A rabbi, Harold
Kushner, has proposed that God is perfectly good and loving, but that
His power is limited; suffering continues because God is not able to
eliminate it.[3] And some thinkers, notably in the Christian Science
movement, have suggested that suffering is illusory, a product of the
human imagination rather than a reality in itself.

Of course, if any of these three positions were correct, then the
religious problem of suffering would disappear. But at what a cost!
For most of us, these alternatives are unacceptable; we are committed,
religiously, to God's power and goodness and to an acknowledgment
of the reality of human suffering.

Several other suggestions concerning theodicy make more sense
and have more claim to being biblical.

One suggestion is that God causes all suffering. He does this for
reasons of His own which are usually not known to us. In any case,
no mere mortal has the right to question God. True faith consists in
unquestioning submission to God's will and in affirming that God has
the sovereign right to do whatever He chooses.

This is a tough-minded position. Doubtless there is some truth in
it, at least in its encouragement to us to be tough-minded rather than
sentimental.

However, I find it an unhelpful position in the end. Even though
it may sometimes be true that God causes suffering, I believe that it
often is the case that God does not cause suffering. People who suffer
are not helped by the suggestion that God is "getting" them. Nor is
this really much of a theodicy; it doesn't really show the justice of
God's actions, but merely insists that we have no right to question

God's actions. This is a misunderstanding of Christian faith. Muslim faith is blind submission to whatever happens, but that is not what Christian faith is. Christian faith is a trusting relationship with God as Friend, Father, Savior, and God; such trust does not demand unquestioning submission but is based on our understanding of God's self-disclosures as a good, loving, and trustworthy God.

Another suggestion is that suffering is inevitable in a world such as ours. For example, if we are to have light, we must have shadows; if we are to have joy, we must have sadness. Similarly, human beings need some physical pain in order to protect them; if fire did not hurt us, we would not know to avoid it. Again, in a natural world suitable for human life, there must be orderliness; gravity must always operate, for example, even when a person falls down and is injured; suffering must be possible. Again, suffering can ennoble human life. Courage, achievement, even love are moral values which could not be possible unless there were evil and suffering to be overcome.

There is something in these comments. In essence, they all say that there is some point to suffering; it contributes something positive to human life and values.

Yet I find these suggestions very limited in their helpfulness. I do not see why there could not be joy in a world without suffering. In fact, I do not see why there could not be joy in a world which did not even have the possibility of suffering. It is true that human beings need some physical pain to protect them, but no one needs all the pain of having bone cancer for years. I accept that the world must function in an orderly manner, that gravity and other regularities of nature are necessary for human life; but what of the suffering caused by the disorderliness of nature, by diseases and by natural disasters, such as storms, earthquakes, and volcanoes? I agree too that suffering can and sometimes does ennoble human beings; but I suspect that far more often it crushes and embitters them.

In brief, while some suffering may serve some valuable purposes, there is a question about whether these purposes justify the suffering; and in any case, vast amounts of human suffering serve no observable purpose.

Perhaps at this point it would be helpful to stipulate as follows: The suffering which troubles our faith in God as our friend and Savior is the pointless suffering of human beings.

The Origin of Suffering

How might a theodicy speak to such pointless suffering? One way is to argue that human beings have brought their suffering on themselves. They are sinners, and sin is the source of all suffering.

This explanation comes in three forms. First, it may stress that we hurt ourselves by our own sin. Second, it may assert that we hurt others by our sin. Third, it may attempt to explain all human suffering in the light of the sin of our first parents.

It is surely true that human beings bring a great deal of suffering on themselves by their sins. A cruel person may end up without a friend in the world; he suffers loneliness because he sinned. A drug addict may bring torment upon himself by his dissipation. A politician may forfeit all her power by dishonest behavior.

I accept the truth of this observation. Much human suffering is deserved. It is difficult to think that God should be blamed for this suffering. Deserved suffering does not pose a barrier to belief that God is good and powerful. In fact, it may actually support this understanding of God to say that He causes those who are cruel and vicious, for example, to suffer for their sins.

So we will stipulate that when people bring suffering on themselves by wrongdoing, such suffering needs no further explanation. But, of course, this is only a fraction of the suffering going on in our world.

Second, much human suffering is caused, not by God, but by other human beings. God should not be blamed for creating a world in which human beings can hurt each other, for only in such a world could human beings ever come to love each other. Further, God should not be blamed for the suffering which is caused by someone, such as Hitler. Hitler was the culprit, not God.

This is certainly a valid point, and it does account for a vast amount of human suffering. And yet, this explanation is not very much help, for this reason: Even though God should not be held responsible for sin and the suffering it causes to others, does He not bear some responsibility to stop it? In 1939 many people of goodwill felt that they were morally obligated to do all that they could to stop Hitler; some gave their lives in the effort. But it does not seem that God used His power and wisdom to stop Hitler. The question which troubles our faith is, Why not?

A third way of speaking of the origin of suffering is to speak of the sin of our first parents. A long tradition in Christian theology suggests that prior to the fall of the human race into sin, no suffering occurred. All suffering is thus somehow related to the sins of our first parents. The story of Adam and Eve (Gen. 2—3) seems to support this view; at first they lived in a beautiful garden but, because of their sin, they were driven from the garden.

There probably is a great deal of truth in this, and I appreciate the help that it provides concerning human suffering. But I also have two questions concerning it.

First, it is very difficult to see any connection between sin and some suffering. Sin may account for the suffering brought on by human guilt or anxiety, for example; but does it account for all the natural disasters and diseases? It is difficult to see how it could.

Second, and closely related, the exact kind of paradise in Eden is not clear. The author of Genesis intended to communicate that things were better before the fall than they were after it; for example, before the fall man had food without labor, but since the fall and, as a consequence of his sin, man must suffer hard labor in order to eat (see Gen. 3:17-19). The question is: What does a person who is suffering need most? Does he need an explanation of where his suffering originated? Or is that, in a sense, largely irrelevant to his personal needs and to his intellectual needs?

The Destiny of Suffering

At this point it would be well for the reader to pause and ask a question: What helps me to cope with suffering? What do I most need during the dark times of life?

I am going to suggest that two things are necessary to me as I face suffering. I think of them both spontaneously during difficult moments. I return to them over and over. I find them both indispensable.

Of course, it is possible that these two things will not be what you readers would need. I offer them as suggestions which may or may not be helpful.

First, I need to know that I am not alone. Second, I need to believe that suffering will not go on forever. Let me explain.

First, I need to know that I am not alone. I need to know that someone is with me and for me, someone who understands and cares. I need to be reassured that I have not been deserted or forgotten. In an illness, I want my doctor to know my name. I want my family to stand by me. I want my friends to care.

And perhaps most of all, I want to know that God cares, that He understands, that He is for me. This is very important to my coping with suffering and to my faith in God.

If no one cared, if none were for me, if God Himself had forgotten me, then suffering would become unbearable. To suffer entirely alone would, I suppose, be hell.

To be loved and supported when we suffer is a very great help. It makes an enormous difference.

But ultimately, it is not enough. I also need something else. I need to believe that suffering is not the ultimate reality. I need to be able to hope for a better time to come, for a time when I will be delivered from my suffering. I need to know that everything that can be done to help me will be done and that God Himself is going to finally provide for my deliverance.

I confess that when I suffer I am not very concerned about why suffering has come to me. I am not concerned about an explanation. A blind man does not want explanations; he wants to see. It is not the origin of suffering that concerns us, but its destiny. We need to know where it is going more than where it has come from. Will it finally be destroyed, or is suffering the final reality?

Now let us notice where our argument has led us. We have recognized that the pointless suffering of relatively innocent persons constitutes a barrier to believing that God is good and loving, powerful and wise. While there are many suggestions concerning theodicy, our deepest religious need is to believe that God cares for us and that in the end He will deliver us from all suffering. If these two things are true, then we can trust God in spite of suffering; but if they are not true, then our trust in God would have to be drastically revised or even forfeited.

Can we believe, then, that God loves us and that He finally will save? What grounds do we have for this trust and hope?

The Crucified God

In many ways God has revealed that He loves us. But the ultimate revelation of His love was given at the cross. And in that event, God also revealed that He understands from the inside what it is to suffer. Jesus is fully sympathetic to us when we suffer. We are never alone. He knows and cares, and He goes through all of our suffering with us.

Furthermore, God revealed in Jesus that He intends to deliver us from all suffering. Just as He raised Jesus from the dead, so He intends to raise us from the dead (see 1 Cor. 15:20). Jesus won a victory over the forces of evil, suffering, and even death; and He has invited humankind to share in the results of His great victory.

In Jesus Christ, our two deepest needs are met concerning suffering. We learn that God understands our suffering and goes with us through it; He is on the side of those who suffer, rather than the cause of their suffering. He is for the victims and not the oppressors. And we also learn that God has won the final victory over suffering and that in the end He will deliver us. Suffering will not have the last word; joy will. (Compare John 16:33.)

In life, some things need to be explained. But some other things do not; they need only to be changed. They do not have an explanation just because they are evil. Some human suffering is like that; it is pointless and undeserved. It cannot be explained, but it can be destroyed. When the final victory over suffering is won, we will have the theodicy we really need: God will be seen to be righteous because He freely accepted the responsibility of delivering humankind from suffering and He provided that deliverance at the cost of great suffering to Himself.

The cross and the resurrection of Jesus give us this hope.

Notes

1. C. S. Lewis, *God in the Dock.*
2. Frederick Sontag, *What Can God Do?*
3. Harold Kushner, *When Bad Things Happen to Good People,* pp. 42-44.

10
Love: Father, Son, and Holy Spirit

How It Was

Before the universe had been created, the Father, the Son, and the Holy Spirit lived together in love. Because their love was perfect, their life together was characterized by uninterrupted happiness or, as we would say today, complete fulfillment.

One day the Father said to the Son and the Spirit, "This love is too good to keep to Ourselves. Let's create some people and share Our love with them."

So they did. And that is how the world began.

The Doctrine of the Trinity

I made up the story above. It is not literally true. But I believe that it points in a true direction, toward a mystery so deep that we need a story such as this one to get at it. The name for that mystery is the Trinity. It is the mystery of the God of love.

I realize that many Christians today probably feel uncomfortable with a story like this one. Why is that?

It is not that they do not know what is meant by the Trinity. Most Christians are familiar with this understanding of God. They are not surprised to hear a reference to Father, Son, and Spirit. They have received the Christian teaching through the baptismal formula (see Matt. 28:19-20), through the Pauline benediction (see 2 Cor. 13:14), and most of all through hymns. It is true that few sermons are preached about the Trinity and few books written. But the vocabulary of the doctrine is familiar to us; we recognize and are familiar with terms such as "one God, three persons" and "Trinity." We know that this understanding of God is traditional in the church; we would recognize and resist the efforts of people who would call it into question.

But still, a story like this one can make us uncomfortable. Most Christians accept the Trinity, but they don't feel comfortable when it is emphasized, and this story emphasizes it. My feeling is that we need to emphasize the doctrine of the Trinity today. Why do I say this? One reason is that it is a universal Christian teaching; that is, it is held by the vast majority of Christians. It also is a distinctively Christian teaching; that is, it has no real parallels in other world religions. So it seems to me that if a story such as this can help us to take the doctrine with more seriousness than usual, it will have been helpful.

We will proceed by attempting to deal very directly with three questions which are asked about the Trinity. The first question is the most basic. It is the question of whether God has really revealed Himself as Father, Son, and Holy Spirit; and if He has, how did He give this revelation? Second, many people are concerned about the reasonableness of the doctrine. Are we contradicting ourselves when we say that God is both one and three? Third, most Christians feel fairly confident that, whatever else may be said, the Trinitarian understanding of God is not very relevant in the day-to-day life and faith of Christians. I shall attempt to refute that assumption.

We shall consider each of these concerns in order.

The Revelation of the Trinity

Through our hymns and our vocabulary, we have received the doctrine of the Trinity which the church worked out by about the fifth century. It is a reasonably clear teaching. It says that there is one God but that He eternally exists as three persons. If we believed, as many of our Roman Catholic friends do, that the traditions of the church were equally as revelatory as the Bible, then it would be quite easy to say that the doctrine of the Trinity is a revealed doctrine.

But many of us do not accept the traditions of the church as revelation. We believe that the Bible is God's written Word and that church traditions are our human efforts to understand the revelation.

So for us the question is, Has God revealed Himself to us as Father, Son, and Holy Spirit in the Bible? I believe that He has, but the form of the revelation is not exactly what we might expect.

When Christians point out that in the New Testament the Father, Son, and Spirit are often mentioned together, they are quite correct. The number of such texts is very large. But that is not the whole story. People who feel hesitant about the doctrine of the Trinity respond by pointing out that the word *Trinity* is not found it the Bible. They also note that God has other names besides Father, Son, and Spirit. They remind us that the Bible does not contain an extended doctrinal discussion of the Trinity. Then they insist that the texts which mention Father, Son, and Spirit are only scattered allusions, and that in building a doctrine on them, we have, in effect, been using them as proof-texts, which is not the wisest way to read the Bible. In all these observations, their views are very perceptive.

But the conclusion which they draw from these observations, namely, that we should give up the doctrine of the Trinity, is incorrect. God has revealed Himself as Trinity in the New Testament, but the form of the revelation is not what these critics were expecting it to be.

We can begin to appreciate the form of the revelation by a candid admission that the texts which speak of the Father, Son, and Spirit are indeed scattered allusions. There are dozens of them. Matthew's Gospel opens and closes with such allusions, and his story of the baptism of Jesus (ch. 4) is very Trinitarian. John's Gospel includes definite Trinitarian references (see 14:16, for example). In Acfs the three persons are mentioned in the sermons preached by the apostles (see Acts 2:17,22, for example). Paul referred often to Father, Son, and Spirit.

These scattered allusions appear in much of the New Testament, and there are many of them. But that is not the remarkable thing about them. The truly remarkable thing is that there is even one such allusion!

We must face this question thoughtfully: How did it ever come about that a Jewish writer spoke of God in terms of threeness? The Jews were fanatically devoted to monotheism; they were deeply committed to the Shema, "Hear, O Israel, the Lord our God is one Lord" (Deut. 6:4). Nothing in the New Testament suggests that any Christian ever challenged that God is one, let alone surrendered that view. Christians believed then as they do now that there is one and only one true and living God.

And yet, they spoke of Father, Son, and Spirit. It is this fact that is so astonishing and that cries out for some explanation.

The explanation is to be found in the religious faith and life of the early Christians. They had a Trinitarian religion. In other words, they worshiped the God of Abraham, Isaac, and Jacob, whom they knew in a new way as the Father of Jesus. Further, they called upon Jesus as their Savior and Lord, and they committed themselves to be His devoted followers. They even prayed to Him and offered Him worship. Further, they believed that the Spirit was with them. They were guided and empowered in their work by the Spirit; and they sensed that He was active in each Christian, providing each one with gifts to use in serving God.

This Trinitarian religious life was natural to the early Christians, and we can hardly imagine what Paul's letters, for example, would look like if this were removed from them. Because they worshiped God, followed Christ, and were led by the Spirit, they found it quite natural to refer to God as Father, Son, and Holy Spirit. That is the explanation for the existence of so many scattered allusions to the Trinity in the New Testament. No other explanation than this seems to me to make sense of these allusions coming from the pens of Jewish monotheists.

But if we have solved the puzzle of the existence of the allusions to the Trinity in the New Testament, we have raised another question. How did the Christians ever come to have a Trinitarian religious life? That is, how did these Jewish people, with their intense loyalty to the God of Israel, come to also follow Jesus and be led by the Spirit?

The answer to this question is much easier to find than the answer to the previous one. How did these people ever come to follow Christ?

The answer is—Christ called them to follow Him. How did they come to be led by the Spirit? The anser is—the Spirit led them.

In other words, because Jesus came and the Spirit was given, people who responded to them religiously began to practice a Trinitarian religious life.

We can put this together as follows. First, God revealed to the Jews that He alone is God and that there is no other. Second, God sent His Son Jesus, who came to be the Savior of the world. Third, God poured out His Spirit on the followers of Jesus on the day of Pentecost.

Those who accepted these historical events as revelations of God moved quite naturally into a Trinitarian religious practice.

Then, when some of these were inspired to write the letters and other writings which we call the New Testament, they quite naturally used Trinitarian language about God.

That is the form of the revelation of God as Father, Son, and Holy Spirit. First came the historical revelation, then the religious experience, and finally the biblical text with its scattered allusions.

The revelation of the Trinity is a very full one indeed. It is quite as fully revealed, for example, as the revelation of the love of God, which also was given first in actions (the cross), experienced by the early Christians (as salvation), and then recorded in the text of the New Testament. If we feel that God's love is revealed to us in the New Testament, then there is no reason to feel that the revelation of the Trinitry is in any way different.

This brings me to comment on a distinction which theologians have made between the economic and essential (or immanent) views of the Trinity. The economic Trinity is God as He has revealed Himself to us in history, in the economy of salvation. The essential Trinity is God as He is in Himself, in His essence. Many Christians have felt comfortable in saying that God is three in the history of salvation, but they have felt that we are not authorized to conclude that God is three within Himself. But the question is, Why will we not make that move? After all, we feel comfortable in thinking that since God has revealed Himself in the economy of salvation to be a God of love, He is in fact a God of love within His own inner life or immanent nature; why then are we unwilling to think that the God who in the economy of salvation revealed Himself to us as three, is also three within His own immanent nature?

Perhaps one reason for the hesitation of many Christians at this point is that they just cannot see the sense of speaking of God as both one and three. To that issue we now turn.

The Reasonableness of the Trinity

We must be very clear now about exactly what we mean by the reasonableness of the doctrine of the Trinity. That phrase does not refer to a revelation of the Trinity; the revelation of the Trinity is found only in the New Testament. Further, I am not now talking about reasons for believing in the Trinity; those also are found only in the New Testament.

Our question now is a much more limited one. We are asking whether the doctrine of the Trinity is self-contradictory. Is it a nonsense idea, such as the idea of a circle with three sides? Is it irrational to believe that there is one God who actually exists as three persons, or is it rather reasonable to believe this?

All Christians agree that belief in the Trinity is a matter of faith. It goes beyond what we could have known about God if He had not revealed Himself to us as such. But does faith in the Trinity constitute a self-contradiction?

The church has always been concerned to express the sense of this doctrine; in other words, we traditionally have believed that the doctrine is not self-contradictory. When Christians first began to defend the doctrine in the fourth and fifth centuries after Christ, they did so by employing philosophical language. They developed a vocabulary, and they used it to show that the teaching was a reasonable one. They were able to convince many of their contemporaries, including many intellectuals, of this.

I have no objection to a philosophical argument for the reasonableness of this doctrine. Perhaps a strong one can still be made.

However, I doubt if many Christians today will find it very helpful. The reason is that most Christians today are not looking for philosophical explanations of Christian doctrine. They are not philosophers, so philosophical explanations do not satisfy them.

Another kind of explanation is needed to show the reasonableness of the Trinity to people today. It is an explanation which has an analogy at its center. It can help us to see the reasonableness of the doctrine that God is both one and three if we can locate an analogy in our experience, a reality familiar to us which is somehow both one and three.

Dozens of such analogies are available and have been used by Christians. A popular one is H_2O which has three forms, solid (ice), liquid (water), and gas (steam). One substance has three distinct forms.

Some people find that this analogy helps them to see the reasonableness of the doctrine that there is one God who exists as Father, Son, and Spirit. I do not find it very helpful, and I can explain why. It is because of my very deep conviction, expressed frequently throughout this book, that God is personal. So important in my understanding of God is this truth, that I do not find it illuminating to think of God in terms of impersonal analogues. And the three forms of H_2O are in fact impersonal analogues. What I would welcome as helpful in an effort to see the reasonableness of the doctrine of the Trinity is a personal analogy, an analogy taken from the realm of persons and interpersonal relations.

When we inquire about personal analogies for the Trinity, we find that the number is reduced from dozens of available ones to two. Either we think of God as three persons or we think of God as one person. If we think of God as three persons, our analogy must somehow show us how God can be one. And if we think of God as one person, our analogy will have to show us how one person is somehow three.

Our natural inclination might be to use the three person analogy, since our traditional language says that God is three persons. But it is not quite that straightforward. For one thing, the New Testament itself does not use the phrase "three persons." The term *person* was first applied to the three by Tertullian (about AD 160-230), who used the Latin *persona,* and it is not altogether clear whether he used it in the sense in which the word *person* is used in modern English. Further, the Greek church fathers (early Christian leaders) did not speak of God as three "persons" (in Greek, that would have been *prosopa*). Rather they spoke of God as three *hypostases,* a word which means something like substances and is sometimes translated "modes of subsistence."

Historically, the church fathers used both analogies. For example, Gregory of Nyssa (about AD 331-396) used the three person analogy in his book entitled *On Not Three Gods,* and Augustine (AD 354-430) used the one person analogy in his book *On the Trinity.* Both of these books are representative of Christian orthodoxy on this doctrine.

Augustine's analogy is sometimes called the psychological analogy. The reason for this name is that he expressed God's threeness in psychological terms. Just as a single person is made up of mind, memory, and will, said Augustine, so the one God is made up of Father, Son, and Spirit.

Gregory's analogy is sometimes called the social analogy because it consists of a small society of three persons. In order to express the unity of three persons as one God, theologians such as Richard of St. Victor have spoken of a bond of love which unites Father, Son, and Spirit.

Both of these analogies have been accepted by the church. Both also can be distorted. The social analogy can be distorted in the direction of tritheism. That is, if it fails to affirm successfully the unity of the three persons, then we are left with three gods.

The psychological analogy can be distorted in the direction of modalism. Modalism is the error which speaks of the Father, Son, and Spirit as temporary modes of God's revelation. It is easy to see why the church has rejected modalism, Christians can hardly be enthusiastic about an understanding of God which speaks of Jesus as no more than a temporary mode of God's self-disclosure.

In my judgment, both of these analogies are useful. Both seem to show us that it is not unreasonable to believe that God is both one and three, since we have analogies for one-and-threeness in our experiences of persons.

Personally I find the analogy of three persons the more helpful. The reason for this is simple. As I read the New Testament, I can think of no more appropriate description of the Father than to say that He is a person; and of the Son, that He is a person. Their relationships are usually interpersonal; God sent, and Jesus came; Jesus prayed, and the Father heard. Further, the Spirit often acts and is acted upon as a person; He teaches, He gives gifts, He is grieved. And frequently He is treated as an equal of the Father and the Son, who clearly are persons.

In other words, the revelation of God's threeness is reasonably clear: the three are persons. It is the unity of God which is mysterious.

Another way to put it is this: God has revealed to us that He is very much like three persons, which leads us to a deeper and more profound understanding of his unity. The inner life of God is characterized by a richness which we never would have suspected; it consists of relationships of love for which the nearest human analogy is the love between persons. We can at least imagine three persons who are so closely united to each other in love that it would be wrong to say of the character of one what we would not say of the others. That is what God is like. Father, Son, and Spirit are bound together in a love so strong that it would be wrong to say of one what we would not say of the others.

Our task was to explore the question of whether it is reasonable to believe that God is both one and three. We said that it would help us to see the reasonableness of this teaching if we could locate an analogy in our experience. We dismissed the nonpersonal analogies as unhelpful, and we said that of the two personal analogies, we found the analogy of three persons the more helpful. Father, Son, and Spirit eternally share a life of love which is so strong that they are one God, not three.

I believe that this analogy is sufficient to show that it is not unreasonable to speak of God as both one and three. If the revelation of God shows that God is three—and it does, as I showed above—then we can accept that revelation without talking nonsense. That is the most that our analogy can do, and it seems to me to do that.

The Relevance of the Trinity

Christians say different things about the Trinity, but many of them would agree about one thing: The Trinity is an abstract teaching with no relevance to real life either in the church or out of it. It seems to me that this is a mistake. I believe that the Trinitarian understanding of God is very relevant to life as well as to thought. I will attempt now to describe its relevance to five areas of concern to Christians.

First, philosophers have long been aware of a logical problem with the Christian doctrine of creation. By definition, God is the ultimate reality. If He has a need to create a world, then He is not perfect; a need would suggest that there was something lacking in God. The creation of the world would then be a matter of importance, but we would be left with a God who was less than we had thought.

On the other hand, if God is perfect and has no need to create the world, then the world does not contribute anything to the ultimate reality. That seems to suggest that the world is in the end a meaningless reality, which is a very discouraging view.

We can put the whole thing another way. If God is personal, He must need to have a personal relationship with someone else, since persons exist always in relationships. But if He does, does that mean that God needs to create persons in order to fulfill Himself? Does that imply an imperfection in God?

It seems to me that the doctrine of the Trinity resolves this problem. It speaks of God as perfect within Himself, as loving and being loved within His own divine life, within His Trinitarian life. God then has no need to create a world. And yet He did create the world, and ourselves in it, in order to have someone upon whom to shower His love. This means that the world is not a meaningless reality at all; God is not toying with us. The world is the object of the love of God.

Second, the doctrine of the Trinity is relevant to Christian theology. It provides us with our most effective way of summarizing what God is like. God is the transcendent Father, the Jesus who lived in history, and the Spirit whom we experience.

Of course, we could speak of God in other terms, but the Trinitarian statement brings together much of what we need to say in a very wonderful way. The early Christians thought so, and that is why their creeds and confessions were frequently structured along Trinitarian lines; the Apostles' Creed is the best-known example. This helps us to appreciate why the Trinity is both a universal Christian teaching and a distinctively Christian teaching about God.

Let's put it the other way around. Could we omit any one of the three persons and still express our faith very well? Could we omit the Father who created the world and sent Jesus? Certainly not. Could we omit the Son who lived among us and died and rose again? Of course not. Could we omit the Spirit who lives in us, who guides and empowers us, and who gives us reassurance and gifts to use in the service of God? No. So, then, we too need a Trinitarian understanding of God when we try to speak theologically.

A third area in which the Trinity is relevant is the gospel. It may seem surprising, but the three persons are mentioned in the basic message which was preached by the earliest church. A good example is Peter's message at Pentecost. He spoke of God who showed His approval of Jesus by giving Him power to do miracles, and who raised Jesus from the dead. Peter also spoke of Jesus, of course, who died and was raised. And he spoke of the Spirit, who empowered Peter to preach and who would be given to all who repented (see Acts 2:22-23,38-39).

It is, of course, possible to preach the gospel effectively and faithfully without referring to the three persons as directly as Peter did. Certainly a message about the gospel is different from a lecture about the Trinity! Nevertheless, behind and beneath the gospel message is a Trinitarian understanding of God, whether or not this is articulated.

Fourth, the Trinity is relevant for Christian living. We are related in a religious way to each of the three persons, just as the early church was. We worship the Father of Jesus and welcome His kingdom. We call upon Jesus as our Lord and Savior and commit ourselves to be

His followers. And we depend upon His Spirit to equip and guide us in our efforts to be God's people in the world. I doubt if any thoughtful Christian would seriously suggest that one or the other of these three religious responses be omitted from our daily lives. In the end, it is probably that fact, more than any other, which will lead us to a deeper appreciation of the doctrine of the Trinity. Only as we come to be conscious of how important each of the three persons is in our daily living, will we become enthusiastic about this doctrine. And that is not a bad thing at all; we do not need to carry around with us a lot of intellectual ideas with no relevance to living. And we should always remind ourselves that the earliest Christians first experienced a Trinitarian religious life, and then they began to speak naturally of God as Father, Son, and Spirit.

Finally, in our worship we find that the language of God as Father, Son, and Spirit is very relevant. No talk about God is as conducive to worship as the Trinitarian language. Perhaps that is why for so long it has been traditional to place the hymn "Holy, Holy, Holy" on the first page of our hymnals.

> Holy, holy, holy! Lord God Almighty!
> Early in the morning our song shall rise to thee;
> Holy, holy, holy! merciful and mighty!
> God in three Persons, blessed Trinity!

When we worship in public or in private, we may discover that the Trinitarian language is more than helpful; we may find that we cannot express our worship without it, that it is indispensable to a fully Christian adoration of God.

Bibliography

Berger, Peter. *A Rumor of Angels.* New York: Doubleday Anchor Books, 1970.

Blair, Joseph. "The Kingdom of God in the Teaching of Jesus." *The Theological Educator* XII (Spring 82):42.

Campenhausen, Hans von. "The Events of Easter and the Empty Tomb." *Tradition and Life in the Early Church,* Philadelphia: Fortress Press, 1968.

Hanson, Anthony. "Symbolism and the Doctrine of God." *London Quarterly and Holborn Review,* July 1964.

Hick, John. *Evil and the God of Love.* London: Fontana Library of Theology and Philosophy, 1970.

Hodgson, Leonard. *And Was Made Man.* London: Longmans, Green, and Co. LTD., 1928.

Klempke, E. D. *The Meaning of Life.* New York: Oxford University Press, 1981.

Kushner, Harold. *When Bad Things Happen to Good People.* New York: Avon Books, 1981.

Lewis, C. S. *God in the Dock.* Michigan: Eerdmans Publishing Company, 1970.

McGiffert, A. C. *The God of the Early Christians.* New York: Scribner's Sons, 1924.

Mackintosh, H. R. *The Christian Apprehension of God.* London: Student Christian Movement Press, 1929.

Moule, C. F. D. *The Origin of Christology.* Cambridge: Cambridge University Press, 1977.

Pannenberg, Wolfhart. *Jesus—God and Man.* Philadelphia: The Westminster Press, MCMLXVIII.

Priestly, J. B. *Instead of the Trees.* New York: Stein and Day, 1977.

Rawlinson, A. E. I. "The Incarnation." *Essays on the Trinity and Incarnation.* London: Longmans, Green and Co., LTD, 1928.

Russell, Bertrand. *Why I am Not a Christian.* New York: Simon and Schuster, 1957.

Sontag, Frederick. *What Can God Do?* Tennessee: Abingdon, 1979.

Tillich, Paul. *Biblical Religion and the Search for Ultimate Reality.* Chicago: University of Chicago Press, 1955.

Webb, C. C. J. *Problems in the Relations of God and Men.* London: Nisbet & Co. LTD., 1924.

Scripture Index